Language and the Teacher:
A Series in Applied Linguistics

Volume 23

under the editorial direction of

DR. ROBERT C. LUGTON

American Language Institute of New York University

LANGUAGE AND THE TEACHER:
A SERIES IN APPLIED LINGUISTICS

The series will be concerned with the following areas—

GENERAL STUDIES
Psycholinguistics, sociolinguistics, bilingualism.

GRAMMAR
Morphology, syntax, contrastive structure.

PHONOLOGY
Phonemics, intonation, contrastive phonetics, etc.

VOCABULARY STUDIES
Frequency counts, production and principles, lexicology.

READING SKILLS
Beginning skills, development, construction of texts, literary reading.

WRITING SKILLS
Beginning skills, development, composition.

METHODOLOGY
Evaluation of methods, techniques, classroom practices.

LANGUAGE TEACHING
FOR DIFFERENT AGE GROUPS
Elementary, secondary, college, adult.

MACHINE TEACHING
Programmed learning, audio-visual equipment and software, language laboratory.

TEACHER EDUCATION
Standards and evaluation, projects, curricula for teacher training

ADMINISTRATION
Curriculum development, articulation, public relations.

TESTING
Techniques, statistical studies.

BIOGRAPHY

BIBLIOGRAPHY

ENGLISH AS A SECOND LANGUAGE

METHODS OF RESEARCH IN LINGUISTICS
AND LANGUAGE TEACHING

Language and the Teacher:
A Series in Applied Linguistics

Current Issues
in
Teaching French

Edited by

Dr. Gaylord Todd

Department of Foreign Languages
University of Nebraska at Omaha

THE CENTER FOR CURRICULUM DEVELOPMENT, INC.

401 Walnut Street   Philadelphia, Pa.

#2786

Contents

Foreword

It seems today beyond serious dispute that linguistics, structural and descriptive, has much to offer the foreign-language teacher from the standpoint both of methodology and of content. The aggressive proselytizing by over-eager linguists and the sometimes equally determined rebuffs by the unconvinced sceptics are now largely a phenomenon of pedagogical and intellectual history. Some exaggerated claims by the linguists have, it is true, been clearly shown to be just that. On the other hand, the basically sound application of the results of the scientific analysis and description of language to the language teaching and learning process has been mutually beneficial for teachers and learners alike. Current developments in the application of linguistic principles to pedagogical problems give promise of substantial additional progress and refinement of methods.

The essays assembled in the volume devoted to *Current Issues in Teaching French* all come from the pens of professionally trained linguistic scientists. They contain, as the perceptive reader will not fail to note, areas of common accord and occasional areas of distinct disagreement. This is a reflection not only of the vigorous debates which continue to be waged among linguistic scientists concerning various theoretical points of procedure and interpretation, but also a reflection of individual differences of outlook and evaluation.

The contributions which follow, then, are offered as a small but significant addition to the growing body of literature on the application of linguistics to the teaching of foreign language in general and French in particular. It is the editor's hope that they will prove as stimulating and informative for the readers of this volume as they have been for him. It is the editor's further hope that the thoughtful pedagogical suggestions contained in these articles will accrue also to the benefit of the students of the readers of this book, on whom the principles enunciated are likely to be tested in actual classroom learning situations.

DR. GAYLORD TODD

SIMON BELASCO*

The Relation of Linguistic Analysis to Foreign-Language Teaching†

At the moment of writing, many colleges and universities have dropped the foreign-language requirement. Certain institutions are seriously considering eliminating all foreign-language courses from their curricula.[1]

This is not the place to determine why after only a decade since the passage of the NDEA Act, the study of foreign language has once more become unpopular. Suffice it to say that the *nature* of the courses offered by most institutions of higher learning is not designed to teach foreign language. Secondary-school teachers take courses in college that have little if anything to do with the language skills they are required to teach in the high school. They never have the opportunity to attain the degree of language proficiency they would like to attain. Nor are they provided with materials that could teach effectively to more than three percent of their students the forty or fifty grammati-

---

* Pennsylvania State University

† Based on the summation address "Language Teaching: Help or Hindrance," presented at the Second International Conference of the Ontario Modern Language Teachers' Association and The New York State Federation of Foreign Language Teachers, Toronto, March 27, 1971.

[1] A case in point is the "Report of the Senate Ad Hoc Committee on Baccalaureate Degree Requirements, Pennsylvania State University," April 23, 1971.

1

cal principles found in standard textbooks. This is true of textbooks using the audiolingual method, the grammar-translation method, or any modified version of either of these two methods.

During the late fifties and early sixties, many educators expected that both structural linguistics and generative linguistics would make valuable contributions to second-language learning. The results did not live up to expectations. Foreign-language methodologists refuse to recognize the almost insurmountable obstacles inherent in an *artificial unicultural* situation represented by the average classroom: (1) individual differences between students, (2) individual differences between teachers, (3) insufficient *time spread* to insure maturation and to prevent reactive inhibition, among others. No one wishes to face the fact that the basic grammatical system, involving syntactic and semantic structure, has never been established or clearly defined for any language.

None of us knows enough about language structure or cognitive processes to design "contrived" materials that will account for individual differences among students. To do the job adequately, contrived materials must be complemented by "live" materials that contain just those semantic, syntactic, and phonological features currently lacking in standard textbooks.[2] These materials must be "controlled;" that is, they must be presented with built-in self-spacing and self-evaluating techniques so that the student can evaluate his own progress and develop at his own speed. I am not talking about programmed learning, mim-mem techniques, or total immersion courses. No one can learn how to speak a foreign language by merely memorizing dialogs and practicing pattern drills. Neither does one learn how to read and comprehend aurally a foreign language by merely reading and listening to foreign-language materials.

One learns to converse in a second language only after one comprehends this language in the mouths of native speakers. Before one can speak, *one must learn how to listen.* When a native speaker addresses a non-native, he watches the latter's facial expressions and *adjusts* his pronunciation and grammar to accommodate the listener. True comprehension can never develop in this fashion. It is absolutely crucial to "overhear" and understand different kinds of natural conversations between second and third parties. And one only learns to speak when the second language is actually being used as a means

---

[2] Simon Belasco, "The Foreign Language Teachers in Search of Values," *Dimensions: Languages '69 Proceedings of the Fifth Southern Conference on Language Teaching*, Atlanta (February 1969), 1-24.

to an end. Real communication is a two-way channel. It subsumes both sending and receiving.[3]

Moreover, to acquire a second language in an artificial situation such as the classroom, the materials must be analyzed *intellectually*. They must be thoroughly discussed in the student's native language to insure an understanding of the grammar and vocabulary of the foreign language. The concept that grammatical principles may be inductively taught, or may be deduced from carefully prepared step-by-step materials, is a myth. The grammatical constraints necessary to insure correct analogizing are not available to foreign-language teachers simply because no one has yet uncovered them. To use an example from English, all of us know that sentences like

      (1) I told something to Bob

              and

      (2) I said something to Bob

are both grammatical. Yet few of us can *intellectualize* why the sentence

      (3) I told Bob something

is grammatical whereas

      (4)* I said Bob something

is not! Note that a *noun containing the feature* [+ *Animate*] *may not directly follow the verb "say."*

The matter is not to be dismissed lightly. It implies a lot of soul-searching self-examination on our part as teachers. How many years did it take each of us to develop one or more skills in the foreign language we are teaching? How many undergraduate and graduate foreign-language majors acquire the four skills: listening, speaking, reading, and writing in any order?

I am *not* implying that drills are useless. There are three sets of features which can be effectively acquired by an audiolingual approach using "assimilation drills" and "testing drills."[4] The first set of features involves the sound system. The second set of features involves the morphophonemic system (e.g., *liaison, élision, sinalefa, sinéresis*), and the third set of features involves basic syntactic structure.[5]

The sound system and the morphophonemic system can be taught

---

[3] Simon Belasco, "Nucleation and the Audio-Lingual Approach," *MLJ*, 49 (December 1965), 482-491.

[4] Simon Belasco and Albert Valdman, *College French in the New Key*, Boston: D. C. Heath, 1965.

[5] Simon Belasco, "Structural Drills and the Refinement Principle," *IJAL*, 29 (April 1963), 19-36.

fairly well along the lines I have outlined elsewhere.[6] I shall not devote too much space to them here. On the other hand, the basic syntactic system has as yet to be defined. The forty to fifty grammatical points found in standard texts include some of the basic structure but certainly not all of it. Most of the standard grammatical points represent intermediate and advanced structure and *cannot be covered actively* in the first two years.

The difference has to be demonstrated between basic "grammatical points" particular to some language, and basic "grammatical theory" applicable to all languages (universal grammar). The former involves such concepts as the use of the subjunctive mood, conjunctive and disjunctive personal pronouns, etc. in French, and the latter the application of the principles of tagmemics, generative grammar, or string constituent analysis to French and other languages.[7]

For French, an example of two basic particular or "idiosyncratic" syntactic points would include the concept of the *verbal-core* involving the use of (1) conjunctive and disjunctive personal pronouns, and (2) the negative *ne . . . pas*. Several weeks, perhaps months, may be required for the average student to master these fundamental principles. Teachers often assume that they may be stated simply and internalized by unrefined drills. The situation is more complex than is commonly supposed.

THE VERBAL-CORE IN NON-EMBEDDED SENTENCES

Observation

Compare the sentences on the left with those on the right. The verbal-core is enclosed within solid lines in each sentence.

1. Ma sœur | regarde | la photo. | Elle la regarde. |
2. Jeanne | a | montré la photo à Jean. | La lui a-t-elle |
                                                           montrée?

---

[6] Simon Belasco, "Toward the Acquisition of Linguistic Competence: From Contrived to Controlled Materials," *MLJ*, 53 (March 1969), 185-205 and "C'est la guerre? Or Can Cognition and Verbal Behavior Coexist in Second Language Learning?," *MLJ*, 54 (October 1970), 395-412.

[7] For tagmemics see Kenneth L. Pike, "On Tagmemes, Née Gramemes," *IJAL*, 24 (1958), 273-278; Robert E. Longacre, "Some Fundamental Insights of Tagmemics," *Language*, 41 (1965), 65-76. For generative grammar see Noam Chomsky, *Syntactic Structures*, The Hague: Mouton and Co., 1957 and *Aspects of the Theory of Syntax*, Cambridge (Mass.): MIT Press, 1965. For string analysis see Zellig S. Harris, *String Analysis of Sentence Structure*, The Hague: Mouton and Co., 1962; Pascal Claris and Naomi Sager, *A String Grammar of French*, New York: Linguistic String Program NYU, 1970.

Discussion

The verbal-core consists of the "conjugated" form of the verb (*regarde; a . . .*) and any conjunctive subject or object pronoun if present (*Elle la regarde; La lui a-t-elle . . .*).

Two Object Pronouns and the Verbal-Core
Two Conjunctive Pronouns

Observation

Compare the sentences on the left with those on the right. The verbal-core is enclosed in solid lines.

1. Jeanne montre la photo à Jean.
2. Jean se rappelle la photo.
3. Jean me présente ses amis.
4. Jeanne envoie les photos au journal.
5. Jean nous montre des photos.
6. Montrez-les à Jeanne.

Jeanne la lui montre.
Jean se la rappelle.
Jean me les présente.
Jeanne les y envoie.
Jean nous en montre.
Montrez-les-lui.

Discussion

Two object pronouns must be conjunctive if at least one of them is *le, la, les, y, en.*

One Conjunctive Pronoun and one Disjunctive Pronoun

Observation

Compare the sentences on the left with those on the right. The verbal-core is enclosed in solid lines.

1. Jeanne me montre à Hélène.
2. Jean se souvient de Paul et de moi.
3. Jean me présente à ses amis.
4. Recommandez-nous à ton patron.

Jeanne me montre à elle.
Jean se souvient de nous.
Jean me présente à eux.
Recommandez-nous à lui.

Discussion

If at least one of two object pronouns cannot be *le, la, les, y, en*—then the direct object is conjunctive and the indirect object is disjunctive.

Ne . . . Pas and the Verbal-Core
Simple Tenses

Observation

Compare the sentences on the left with those on the right. The verbal-core is enclosed in solid lines.

1. ⌐Ecoutez !⌐   N' ⌐écoutez⌐ pas!

2. ⌐Ecoutez-le!⌐   Ne ⌐l'écoutez⌐ pas!

3. Jeanne ⌐écoute.⌐   Jeanne n' ⌐écoute⌐ pas.

4. Jeanne ⌐écoute⌐ sa mère.   Elle ⌐ne l'écoute⌐ pas.

5. Est-ce qu' ⌐elle l'écoute?⌐   Ne ⌐l'écoute-t-elle⌐ pas?

Discussion

To make a sentence negative, place *ne (n')* after the subject if it comes first. Otherwise *ne (n')* comes first. *Pas* is placed at the end of the verbal-core.

COMPOUND TENSES

Observation

Compare the sentences on the left with those on the right. The verbal-core is enclosed in solid lines.

1. Jeanne ⌐a⌐ écouté la radio.   Jeanne n' ⌐a⌐ pas écouté.

2. Jeanne ⌐l'a⌐ écoutée.   Jeanne ne ⌐l'a⌐ pas écoutée.

3. ⌐Elle l'a⌐ écoutée.   Elle ⌐ne l'a⌐ pas écoutée.

4. ⌐L'a-t-elle⌐ écoutée?   Ne ⌐l'a-t-elle⌐ pas écoutée?

Discussion

For compound tenses, the negative rule is the same. Note that *pas* occurs before the past participle.

These rules represent "closed rules;" that is, they are relatively complete and non-contradictory. Closed rules are part of the basic syntactic structure. Rules such as the negative rule in standard textbooks may appear to be more simple, but they are neither complete nor non-contradictory, e.g., "place *ne* in front of the verb and *pas* after the verb." One or two examples will clearly show that the latter "rule" is incorrect:

(5) *Ne* la montre-t-elle *pas?*

(6) Elle *ne* l'a *pas* montrée.

In neither sentence does *ne . . . pas* bear this relation to the "verb". In sentence (5) *ne* precedes the object pronoun and *pas* follows the subject pronoun. In sentence (6) *ne* precedes the subject pronoun and *pas* follows the auxiliary.

Tagmemic theory has received widespread practical application to second-language learning in the form of "substitution drills." Generative, or more nearly transformation, theory has inspired "correlation drills" and "conversion drills." It is commonly assumed that linguistic behavior is habitual and that a language may be acquired by internalizing certain structural patterns through intensive practice. Although every foreign-language textbook during the past ten years seems to have subscribed to this tenet, the obvious dearth of "internalized" foreign-language students in high school and college readily attests otherwise.

Let us assume that all the sentences in the French language are derived from three basic sentence types, more nearly from the structure underlying these basic types.[8] This may represent a universal principle; that is, this assumption may hold for the sentences of all languages. The following "basic frames" will help to illustrate the concept for French sentences:

> *a.* Jean parle   (maintenant).
> *b.* Jean parle anglais   (maintenant).[9]
> *c.* Jean est anglais   (maintenant).

Frame *a* consists of two obligatory slots S(ubject), P(redicator) and an optional slot A(dverbial). Frames *b* and *c* are each composed of three obligatory slots, S, P, C(complement) and one optional slot A. The letters S, P, C, A represent syntactic relational positions or points in the clause where different fillers (words) may be interchanged (substituted).

>   S   P   (A)
> *a.* Jean parle   (maintenant).
>   S   P   C   (A)
> *b.* Jean parle anglais (maintenant).
>   S   P   C   (A)
> *c.* Jean est anglais (maintenant).

Frame *a* has no C slot, and it is this feature which distinguishes it

---

[8] First discussed in Simon Belasco, editor, *Manual and Anthology of Applied Linguistics*, University Park, Pa.: Nittany Press, 1960; *Applied Linguistics: French, German, Italian, Russian, Spanish*, 5 vols., Boston: D. C. Heath, 1961. Revised versions of the General and French Sections have been published as Simon Belasco and Albert Valdman, *Applied Linguistics and The Teaching of French*, University Park, Pa.: Nittany Press, 1968.

[9] More specifically, Frame *b* is rendered as *Jean parle [français / à Marie]*, where this frame is said to take a direct object and/or a non-direct object.

from Frames *b* and *c*. To put it differently, Frames *b* and *c* each has a C slot, whereas Frame *a* does not. On the other hand, the C slot in Frame *c* contains a filler that functions as a S(ubjective) A(ttribute), whereas in *b* the filler functions as a D(irect) O(bject) and/or N(on-Direct) O(bject).

In other words, in Frame *a*, the P slot contains an In(transitive) verb, in *b* a Tr(ansitive) verb, and in *c* a link-verb or Cop(ula). Thus, it is the *verb* that indicates in each instance how the clause functions in actual discourse.[10] Moreover, the verb type in the P slot automatically determines the function of the filler in the S slot. In Frames *a* and *b*, the filler functions as an Act(or).[11] In *c*, it functions as an Eq(uatant) since the link-verb puts the filler in the S slot in equational relation with the filler in the C slot.

Thus, each syntactic slot (S, P, C, A) contains a filler which has a specific function.[12]

$$
\begin{array}{llll}
\text{S} & \text{P} & & \text{(A)} \\
\text{Act}_{(in)} & \text{In} & & \text{(Tem)} \\
\end{array}
$$
a. Jean parle (maintenant).

$$
\begin{array}{llll}
\text{S} & \text{P} & \text{C} & \text{(A)} \\
\text{Act}_{(tr)} & \text{Tr} & \text{DO} & \text{(Tem)} \\
\end{array}
$$
b. Jean parle anglais (maintenant).

$$
\begin{array}{llll}
\text{S} & \text{P} & \text{C} & \text{(A)} \\
\text{Eq} & \text{Cop} & \text{SA} & \text{(Tem)} \\
\end{array}
$$
c. Jean est anglais (maintenant).

It follows then that the vertical column of features forms a unit:

slot
|
function
|
filler

This unit is known as a "tagmeme" on the clause level. Usually tagmemes are identified by the simple designation "functional slot":

---

[10] Simon Belasco, "Les structures grammaticales orales," *Le Français dans le Monde*, 41 (June 1966), 37-48.

[11] The term "Subject as Actor" is a cover term for the subject functioning as "semantic" agent, patient, experiencer, benefactor, instrument, etc. in the active voice.

[12] The filler in slot C may function as a direct object (DO), non-direct object (NO), subjective complement or attribute (SA), or objective complement (OC). NO may be subcategorized as an indirect object (IO), passive agentive (Ag), locative (LOC), etc. The filler in slot A may function as an adverbial of time (Tem), frequency (Freq), place (Pl), duration (Dur), direction (Dir), manner (Man), measure (Meas), etc.

S, Act$_{(in)}$; P, In; etc. Strictly speaking, the horizontal combination of tagmemes designates the sentence type or "hypertagmeme" (basic frame). It should be noted that the filler in any given slot may be a single word or a word-group (phrase).

Thus, the phrase *Ton cousin Jean* or *Ton cousin* might function as a S, Act$_{(tr)}$ tagmeme in the slot containing the single word *Jean* in Frame *b* above. In the same way, the phrase *a dû parler* or *venait de parler* can function as a P, Tr tagmeme instead of the single word *parle*. Furthermore, by replacing the word *anglais* by the phrase *une langue étrangère* and *maintenant* by *ce matin*, we have a variant of Frame *b* which looks like this:

$$
\begin{array}{ll}
\textbf{S} & \textbf{P} \\
\text{Act} & \text{Tr} \\
(\textbf{tr}) & \\
\end{array}
$$

b. Ton cousin Jean / a dû parler /

$$
\begin{array}{ll}
\textbf{C} & (\textbf{A}) \\
\text{DO} & (\text{Tem}) \\
\end{array}
$$

une langue étrangère / ce matin.

This clause consists of four tagmemes, three of which (S, Act$_{(tr)}$ / C, DO / A, Tem) contain a noun phrase, and one (P, Tr) a verb phrase.

The pedagogical application in the form of a substitution drill goes something like this. A sentence is presented orally as a "base." The student repeats the sentence. Then a different noun-phrase or verb-phrase is presented as a cue,[13] which the student substitutes for one of the phrases in the base. If the drill is designed correctly, the cue should fit in only one slot. For example, if the base happens to be

$$
\begin{array}{lll}
\textbf{S} & \textbf{P} & \textbf{C} \\
\end{array}
$$

Les Américains / regardent / les Françaises

the cue *les piétons* might be given, which can fit either in slot S or slot C. This is to be avoided, otherwise a "breakdown" may occur later on in the drill. A cue such as *les photos* is more appropriate since it can only fit in the C slot. Executed in this fashion, the various items substituted are more readily controlled.

Several kinds of changes may occur in a given slot of the base: (a) modification, (b) extension, (c) replacement, or (d) reduction. For example, the entry *Jean* in Frame *b* may be "modified" by the

---

[13] The terms noun-phrase and verb-phrase used here are not co-extensive with the terms NP and VP of generative transformational grammar.

cue *Jeannot*, "extended" by *Ton cousin Jean*, or simply "replaced" by *Ton cousin*. In like fashion, the entry *Ton cousin Jean* may subsequently be "reduced" to *Jean*.

The members of a noun-phrase make up a construction known as a "structure of qualification." The same is true of a verb-phrase, adjective-phrase, or adverb-phrase. The tagmemes in each of the Frames *a, b, c* that follow contain a phrase that has a "head-word" (noun, verb, adjective, adverb) and a qualifier or "marker."

S	P		(A)
$Act_{(in)}$	In		(Freq)
d 1	aux 2		(i) (4)
a. Ton cousin /	a parlé /		(assez souvent).

S	P	C	(A)
$Act_{(tr)}$	Tr	DO	(Freq)
d 1	aux 2	d 1	(i) (4)
b. Ton cousin /	a parlé /	cette langue /	(assez souvent).

S	P	C	(A)
Eq	Cop	SA	(Freq)
d 1	aux 2	i 3	(i) (4)
c. Ton cousin /	peut être /	très embêtant /	(assez souvent).

We can use Frame *c* as a test frame to identify the four parts of speech functioning as a head-word. The word *cousin* is a noun (1) because it is marked by a d(eterminer) *ton*; *être* is a verb (2) because it is marked by an aux(iliary) *peut*; *embêtant* is an adjective (3) because it is marked by the i(ntensifier) *très* and at the same time functions as SA; *souvent* is an adverb (4) because it is the only head-word that may optionally occur at the beginning and end of a frame or between slots P and C. Note, in passing, that the intensifier *assez* makes the filler in the A slot a structure of qualification as does each marker in the S, P, and C slots.

We can therefore consider each structure of qualification in a clause slot as composed of two or more slots on the "phrase level."

S			P	
$Act_{(in)}$			In	
d 1 3			aux 2	
(7) Les / Anglais / enragés //			ont / avancé.	

Such an analysis has pedagogical import when treating morphophonemic phenomena such as *liaison* in French. For example, *liaison* may be (1) obligatory, (2) optional, or (3) forbidden, depending on the position of a qualifier in relation to its head-word or some other head-word. Thus in sentence 7, *liaison* is obligatory between a noun beginning with a vowel sound and a "preceding" qualifier ending in a latent consonant (Les͜Anglais).[14] It generally seems that the possibility of *liaison* is greater when a qualifier "precedes" rather than "follows" a head-word. All the words in sentence 7 end in a latent consonant and, except for *Les*, all the words begin with a vowel sound. Except between *Les* and *Anglais* where it is obligatory, *liaison* is potentially optional between any two words in the sentence—but in varying degrees—depending on the style.[15]

In fast colloquial speech, optional *liaison* is rarely made. In careful speech, optional *liaison* is made between the "preceding" qualifier auxiliary and the verb in the P slot (ont͜avancé). In oratorical style, optional *liaison* is made between the plural noun head-word and a following qualifier (Anglais͜enragés). And in reciting poetry, all optional *liaisons* are made—even between words in contiguous clause slots (enragés͜ont).

The elements making up the verbal-core have a high degree of cohesion, and *liaison* is obligatory between all of the elements—always cutting across clause slot boundaries.

```
S        P
Ils͜ont  avancé.
S        P
On͜a     avancé.
S    C         P
Elles nous͜ont attaqués.
```

However, with elements outside the verbal-core, the degree of cohesion is lower. *Liaison* is "optional" between the preceding auxiliary and the past participle (ont͜avancé, ont͜attaqués), and "forbidden" between any post verbal-core 3d person pronoun and a following word beginning with a vowel.[16]

```
Ont-ils / avancé?
A-t-on / avancé?
Nous ont-elles / attaqués?
Donnez-en / aux troupes.
```

---

[14] French words terminating in final unpronounced consonants: *s, z, x, t, d, n, r, p, g* are said to be "latently" realized (linked) in *liaison*.

[15] For a discussion of stylistic variation in *liaison*, see Pierre Delattre, *Principes de phonétique française*, Middlebury, 1951, pp. 26-34.

[16] *Liaison* is, however, optional between post verbal-core 1st and 2d person plural pronouns and a following word beginning with a vowel: *Irons-nous ↓ au cours? Qu'avez-vous ↓ entendu?*

Now these principles are not readily assimilated by the average student. Drills designed to develop correct morphophonemic "habits" involve a lot of detailed planning, to say nothing of the many hours of student practice required for internalization of the principles in question. Morphophonemic principles can be taught effectively over a long period of time with so-called assimilation and testing drills. On the other hand, it is doubtful if a worthwhile number of grammatical principles can be successfully internalized by pattern practice. I shall say more about this later.

In any event, it is not difficult to understand the pedagogical import of the grammatical analysis that has been outlined thus far. It is primarily designed to teach language by manipulating the related elements of grammatical constructions.

Basically, there are two types of assimilation replacement drills (simple substitution, progressive substitution) and two types of testing replacement drills (simple correlation, progressive correlation). The exercises on pages 13-15 illustrate each of these types. It is assumed that the student has already been presented with an "intellectual" analysis of the non-definite determiners: indefinite and partitive articles.

Simple substitution and progressive substitution drills are designed to teach basic vocabulary. Simple substitution is too mechanical a drill. It requires no reflection on the part of the student. Not only can this drill result in boredom, but the student can execute it without having the slightest idea of the meaning of the cue. Some of the disadvantages associated with SS drills can be overcome by keeping them short. Progressive substitution demands more attention from the student since he must be careful to substitute different kinds of cues in more than one slot. A PS drill serves to review the grammatical principle being "assimilated" and acts as a transitional exercise before the testing drills are employed. It is important to note that the cues used in SS and PS drills only replace certain words and do not "change" the other elements in the construction in any way.

With testing drills, the situation is different. The cue that is inserted in a simple correlation drill or a progressive correlation drill either undergoes a change, or causes a change in the words of the same or neighboring slot. (See pages 16 and 17.)

Thus correlation drills are designed to determine or test if the basic structure has been "internalized". If the substitution drills have not done their work, the correlation drills will reveal this immediately. And this happens far too frequently. To remedy this, the student is asked to repeat the substitution drills or is presented with additional

Practice: **The use of the non-definite determiners with count nouns (*un, une, des*) and with mass nouns (*du, de la, de l'*).**

1. SIMPLE SUBSTITUTION (SS)

a. COUNT NOUNS

Masculine Singular

BASE SENTENCE	CUES	RESPONSES
1. Il a acheté un fauteuil.		1. Il a acheté un fauteuil.
2.	un lit	2. Il a acheté un lit.
3.	un frigo	3. Il a acheté un frigo.
4.	un téléviseur	4. Il a acheté un téléviseur.
5.	un magnétophone	5. Il a acheté un magnétophone.

Feminine Singular

BASE SENTENCE	CUES	RESPONSES
1. Il va acheter une table.		1. Il va acheter une table.
2.	une chaise	2. _____ une chaise.
3.	une lampe	3. _____ une lampe.
4.	une radio	4. _____ une radio.
5.	une voiture	5. _____ une voiture.

Masculine and Feminine Plural

BASE SENTENCE	CUES	RESPONSES
1. Il a trouvé des fauteuils.		1. Il a trouvé des fauteuils.
2.	des lits	2. _____ des lits.
3.	des chaises	3. _____ des chaises.
4.	des lampes	4. _____ des lampes.
5.	des tables	5. _____ des tables.

b. MASS NOUNS

Masculine Pre-consonantal

BASE SENTENCE	CUES	RESPONSES
1. Elle a cherché du fromage.		1. Elle a cherché du fromage.
2.	du lait	2. _____ du lait.
3.	du beurre	3. _____ du beurre.
4.	du café	4. _____ du café.
5.	du vin	5. _____ du vin.

Feminine Pre-consonantal

BASE SENTENCE	CUES	RESPONSES
1. Elles ont mangé de la salade.		1. Elles ont mangé de la salade.
2.	de la soupe	2. _____ de la soupe.
3.	de la viande	3. _____ de la viande.
4.	de la fondue	4. _____ de la fondue.
5.	de la glace	5. _____ de la glace.

Masculine and Feminine Pre-vocalic

BASE SENTENCE	CUES	RESPONSES
1. Ils ont demandé de l'argent.		1. Ils ont demandé de l'argent.
2.	de l'ail	2. _____ de l'ail.
3.	de l'alcool	3. _____ de l'alcool.
4.	de l'eau	4. _____ de l'eau.
5.	de l'aspirine	5. _____ de l'aspirine.

2. PROGRESSIVE SUBSTITUTION (PS)

COUNT AND MASS NOUNS

Mixed Drill

BASE SENTENCE	CUES	RESPONSES
1. Ils ont choisi une voiture.		1. Ils ont choisi une voiture.
2.	un fauteuil	2. _____ un fauteuil.
3.	Ils ont acheté	3. _____
4.	des lampes	4. _____ des lampes.
5.	Elles ont choisi	5. _____
6.	du fromage	6. _____ du fromage.
7.	Il a demandé	7. _____
8.	de la soupe	8. _____ de la soupe.
9.	Elle a apporté	9. _____
10.	de l'eau	10. _____ de l'eau.

3. SIMPLE CORRELATION (SC)

a. COUNT NOUNS

Masculine and Feminine Singular

BASE SENTENCE	CUES	RESPONSES
1. Il a acheté un fauteuil.		1. Il a acheté un fauteuil.
2.	lampe	2. _____ une lampe.
3.	téléviseur	3. _____ un téléviseur.
4.	frigo	4. _____ un frigo.
5.	radio	5. _____ une radio.
6.	lit	6. _____ un lit.

b. MASS NOUNS

Masculine and Feminine Singular

BASE SENTENCE	CUES	RESPONSES
1. Elle a cherché du fromage.		1. Elle a cherché du fromage.
2.	ail	2. _____ de l'ail.
3.	fondue	3. _____ de la fondue.
4.	eau	4. _____ de l'eau.
5.	soupe	5. _____ de la soupe.
6.	beurre	6. _____ du beurre.

4. PROGRESSIVE CORRELATION (PC)

COUNT AND MASS NOUNS

Masculine and Feminine Singular

BASE SENTENCE	CUES	RESPONSES
1. Ils ont apporté une table.		1. Ils ont apporté une table.
2.	ail	2. _____ de l'ail.
3.	mangé	3. Ils ont mangé _____
4.	viande	4. _____ de la viande.
5.	acheté	5. Ils ont acheté _____
6.	frigo	6. _____ un frigo.
7.	demandé	7. Elles ont vendu _____
8.	radio	8. _____ une radio.
9.	cherché	9. Ils ont cherché _____
10.	beurre	10. _____ du beurre.

Masculine and Feminine Partitive

BASE SENTENCE	CUES	RESPONSES
1. Elles ont choisi des lampes.		1. Elles ont choisi des lampes.
2.	l'argent	2. _____ de l'argent.
3.	apporté	3. Elles ont apporté _____
4.	chaises	4. _____ des chaises.
5.	acheté	5. Elles ont acheté _____
6.	lait	6. _____ du lait.
7.	vendu	7. Elles ont vendu _____
8.	viande	8. _____ de la viande.
9.	demandé	9. Elles ont demandé _____
10.	tables	10. _____ des tables.

ones. Language skills are hard to come by in the ordinary classroom situation. Even if the student executes the drills perfectly, there is little guarantee that he will use the principle properly in a natural context.

There is one more kind of structure of qualification that has not been mentioned, one involving the P and A slots. The following clause is not Frame *b* but Frame *a*.

$$S \qquad P \qquad (A)$$

a. Le sac / pèse / vingt livres.

The phrase *vingt livres* functions as an adverbial of measure and modifies the verb *pèse*, making the PA slots a structure of qualification. If the filler in the S slot is replaced by an entry having the feature [+ Human], then the clause becomes ambiguous and may be either Frame *a* or Frame *b*.

$$S \qquad P \qquad (A)$$

a. Le garçon / pèse / vingt livres.

$$S \qquad P \qquad C$$

b. Le garçon / pèse / vingt livres.

In the given context, the filler *vingt livres* could mean "twenty pounds" or "twenty books". In Frame *a, vingt livres* is replaced by the pro-adverb *tant* (*Le garçon pèse tant*). In Frame *b, vingt livres* is replaced by the pro-noun *les* (*Le garçon les pèse*) making the PC slots a structure of complementation not qualification. There are also pro-verbs and pro-adjectives, but little else will be said about these pro-forms here.

Verbs such as *peser, courir, vivre, coûter,* etc., are often called mid-verbs because they may function otherwise than transitively or intransitively. Their function depends frequently on the type of filler in the A and C slots. By means of transformation—more nearly "conversion"—drills, it is possible to illustrate a three-way function for the verb *courir*.

SAMPLE CONVERSION

$$S \qquad P \qquad C$$

Transitive: a. Il a couru ces dangers →
Ces dangers qu'il a courus.

$$S \qquad P \qquad (A)$$

Mid: b. Il a couru vingt minutes →
Les vingt minutes qu'il a couru.

S   P   (A)

Intransitive: c. Il a couru le matin → ∅

Conversion of the first frame shows that the past participle agrees with the preceding direct object (*qu'*), *qu'il a courus* being a relative clause. Conversion of the second frame results in the qualifying clause *qu'il a couru*,[17] where the past participle remains invariable. This failure to agree is characteristic of mid-verbs. No conversion is possible for the third frame since the filler *le matin* cannot function as an antecedent of a relative or a qualifying clause. The symbol ∅ indicates that conversion cannot take place.

By combining them with other frames, it is possible to illustrate how these three frames may be incorporated in a drill.

MULTIPLE CONVERSION

BASE SENTENCES   RESPONSES

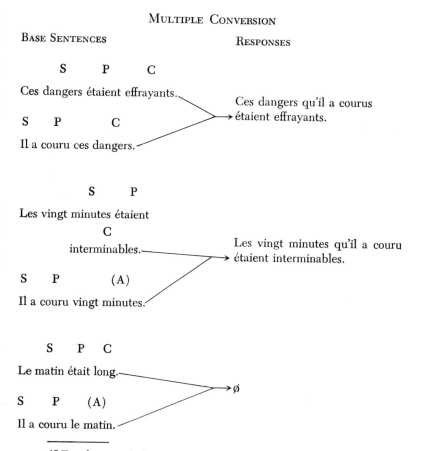

S   P   C

Ces dangers étaient effrayants.

S   P   C

Il a couru ces dangers.

→ Ces dangers qu'il a courus étaient effrayants.

S   P

Les vingt minutes étaient

C

interminables.

S   P   (A)

Il a couru vingt minutes.

→ Les vingt minutes qu'il a couru étaient interminables.

S   P   C

Le matin était long.

S   P   (A)

Il a couru le matin.

→ ∅

---

[17] For the use of this construction in writing, see Maurice Grevisse, *Le bon usage*, 8th ed., Gembloux: J. Duculot, 1964, pp. 716-718.

Used with a mid-verb like *courir*, the filler *vingt minutes* is an adverbial of measure not an adverbial of time, as in the case of *le matin*. It is this property of adverbials of measure (weight, price, duration, value, distance, etc.) that makes them function "almost" as direct objects and are often designated as "pseudo-accusatives."

Frames *a, b, c* either individually or in combination with one another may be converted into one or more "non-basic" sentences. For example, some sentence may occur in the passive voice, which changes its status from a basic to a non-basic Frame *b*.[18]

S   P   C

$Act_{(tr)}$ Tr   DO

(8) *Le camion / a renversé / l'homme* →

S   P   C

Go   Pas   Ag

(9) *L'homme / a été renversé / par le camion.*

Thus by transposing and adding to the original structure, it is possible to manipulate the words within a slot or between slots, thereby changing their function. In sentences 8 and 9 the S, P, C slots occur in the same order, but *l'homme* originally in the C, DO slot is now in the S, Go(al) slot; *le camion* which was in the S, $Act_{(tr)}$ slot is in the C, Ag(ent) slot and is preceded by *par;* the words *a renversé* in the P, Tr slot are now in a P, Pas slot and the auxiliary *été* has been placed between them.

In the same way, a basic Frame *b* and a basic Frame *c* can be combined and converted into a non-basic Frame *b* sentence containing an O(bjective) C(omplement).

S   P   C

$Act_{(tr)}$ Tr   DO

(10)   *On*   *nomme Jean.*

S   P   C   C

$Act_{(tr)}$ Tr   DO   OC

→ (12)   *On*   *nomme Jean chef.*

S   P   C

Eq   Cop   SA

(11) *Jean est chef.*

---

[18] Non-basic frames are also called "altered" frames. For a treatment of this feature, see Belasco and Valdman, *Applied Linguistics . . .* , pp. 40-42.

In this instance, the S, Eq and the P, Cop slots containing the fillers *Jean* and *est* respectively of sentence 11 are deleted, and the C, SA slot containing the filler *chef* becomes the C, OC slot of sentence 12.

Conversion exercises like correlation drills are designed to test the student's acquisition of the basic structure. They may be sub-categorized as "simple" and "multiple" conversion drills.[19]

SIMPLE CONVERSION

Testing Drill: Transpose to the passive voice where possible.

BASIC SENTENCES	RESPONSES
1. La vendeuse pèse les poires.	→ Les poires sont pesées par la vendeuse.
2. La pluie dure trois jours.	→ $\emptyset$[20]
3. Le médecin soigne l'enfant.	→ L'enfant est soigné par le médecin.
4. Le colis pèse quarante grammes.	→ $\emptyset$
5. Les piétons courent ce matin.	→ $\emptyset$
6. L'inspecteur interroge les hommes.	→ Les hommes sont interrogés par l'inspecteur.

MULTIPLE CONVERSION

Testing Drill: Combine frames to form objective complement constructions.

BASIC SENTENCES   RESPONSES

1. a. Le directeur nomme Jean.

       Le directeur nomme Jean instituteur.

   b. Jean est instituteur.

2. a. Le peuple juge les prisonniers.

       Le peuple juge les prisonniers coupables.

   b. Les prisonniers sont coupables.

---

[19] It should be emphasized that these "conversions" are pedagogical exercises and do not necessarily correspond to "transforms" found in generative grammar. The *meaning* of the sentences thus converted is not at issue here. What is relevant is whether or not the structure on the right when "derived" from the structure on the left is a grammatical structure. In other words, conversions do not imply that the structures on the left are necessarily the deep structures that underlie the structures on the right.

[20] In an oral drill, instead of responding "zero," the student may repeat the structure on the left, i.e., *La pluie dure trois jours,* to indicate that this sentence does not undergo conversion.

3. a. Les bandits proclament Robin.

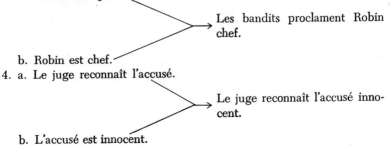

Les bandits proclament Robin chef.

  b. Robin est chef.

4. a. Le juge reconnaît l'accusé.

Le juge reconnaît l'accusé innocent.

  b. L'accusé est innocent.

Not all conversions prove to be this simple. More complex types occur illustrated as follows with the verb *faire* used as a "causative".

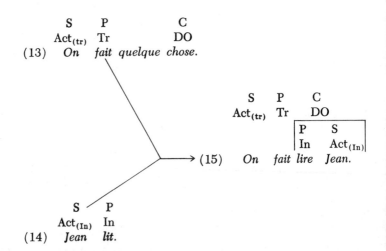

Unlike sentence 10, the C, DO in sentence 13 does not contain the filler *Jean*. In other words, no one "makes" *Jean* (except God or his parents). Sentence 15 is the result of embedding sentence 14 in the C, DO slot of sentence 13. The conversion replaces the "dummy" filler *quelque chose* by the fillers *Jean* and *lit*. The latter are reversed and *lit* assumes the infinitive form. Note that *Jean* still functions as S, Act$_{(In)}$ and *lire* as P, In, but both fillers are in the C, DO slot of sentence 13. Note also that if we add a C, DO slot to sentence 14, the functions of *Jean* and *lit* remain the same although other changes may occur. Consider the next two examples.

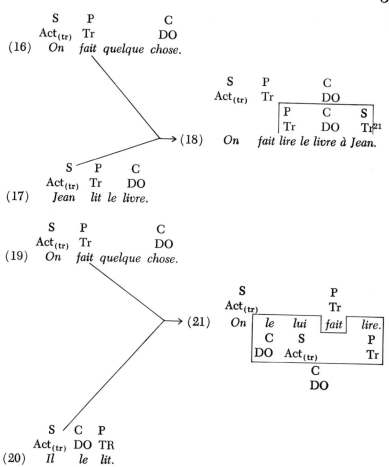

```
        S      P              C
      Act(tr)  Tr             DO
(16)    On    fait quelque chose.

                                      S      P          C
                                    Act(tr)  Tr         DO
                                              ┌──────────────────────┐
                                              │ P     C     S        │
                                              │ Tr    DO    Tr       │²¹
                                              └──────────────────────┘
                                  (18)  On   fait lire le livre à Jean.

            S    P    C
          Act(tr) Tr  DO
(17)      Jean  lit le livre.

        S      P              C
      Act(tr)  Tr             DO
(19)    On    fait quelque chose.

                                      S                    P
                                    Act(tr)                Tr
                                  ┌──────────────────────────────────┐
                         (21) On  │ le    lui   │ fait │  lire.       │
                                  │ C     S     │      │  P           │
                                  │ DO  Act(tr) │      │  Tr          │
                                  └──────────────────────────────────┘
                                              C
                                              DO

        S  C  P
      Act(tr) DO TR
(20)   Il  le lit.
```

Sentence 17 is embedded in the C, DO slot of sentence 16. The filler *lit* is infinitivized as *lire* and placed in initial posititon in the slot. Then follow the direct object *le livre* and the subject *Jean* preceded by *à*. Note that the sequence *à Jean* does not represent an indirect object despite the presence of *à*. The form *à* is a marker and serves to distinguish the subject *Jean* from the direct object *le livre*.²²

---

²¹ This sentence is of course ambiguous and may mean either "We have someone read the book to John," or "We have John read the book" ("We have the book read by John"). To avoid confusion, many French speakers render this sentence as *On fait lire le livre par Jean.*

²² Compare this to the use of *a* in Spanish to distinguish the subject from the object: *El perro ve al gato,* "The dog sees the cat"; *Al perro ve el gato,* "The cat sees the dog."

In like fashion, sentence 20 is embedded in the C, DO slot of sentence 19. We now have an instance of a discontinuous slot or "slot splitting". The filler *lit* is infinitivized as *lire* and placed to the right of the main verb *fait*. The subject of the infinitive *lui* is placed to the left of *fait*. Again the form *à* is contained in the subject pronoun *lui*—resulting from the fusion of *à* plus *il*—and serves to distinguish it from the preceding direct object *le*.

This analysis of causative *faire* sentences is different from that found in standard textbooks. It emphasizes the functional relations between the elements of the main sentence and the embedded sentence, thereby helping the student to understand so-called "anomalous" constructions.

Now it may seem that the kinds of drills we have been discussing here would account for the "production" of many sentences. Actually the benefit derived from training and practice using this technique is limited to the perception and production of certain sound combinations and the most elementary of syntactic structures. The creation of an indefinite—if not infinite—number of *new* sentences resulting from the internalization of a long chain of abstract interpretive rules could never be effected in this manner. Drills will not guarantee anything! Even accompanied by intellectual analysis, they can only create a "state of expectancy" or "awareness" of what must be internalized eventually in order for the student to develop the four skills. By "eventually" I do not mean the first year, the second year, the third year, or the fourth year. Astonishing as it may sound, by "eventually" I mean anywhere from a six-to-thirteen-year period depending on the second-language acquisition potential of the language learner.

Primacy must be given to *listening* and *reading*. This does not preclude practicing "speaking," but let us not delude ourselves that we are teaching true verbal production. We are training our students to "vocalize," and this kind of "speaking" must be accompanied in great depth by the acquisition of the listening skill. The drills we have been describing represent "contrived" materials. They can only teach basic structure. They may be a "necessary" condition for learning a language in an artificial unicultural situation, but they are far from "sufficient." Only by working with "live" listening and reading materials can the student be brought into contact with the structure and vocabulary existing in the "real" world. Once this "real" structure and vocabulary are intellectualized and internalized, then and only then can "real" language proficiency develop.

Once the student has acquired the basic structure, he should be exposed to self-pacing, self-evaluating *controlled* materials. These materials are the actual written and oral texts encountered by any native speaker of a foreign language: novels, stories, newspaper articles, radio and televised broadcasts, taped interviews, sound tracks of films, etc.

The student begins with a few lines of oral or written French *accompanied by the English equivalent.* He reads the English first to grasp the concept, i.e., the *meaning,* of what he is to hear or read in French. He "analyses" the French text to determine if he knows "who (or what) does what to whom (or to what), for whom, with what—how, when, where, why." For example, John (or Fido) takes the newspaper to Mary (or to Lassie) for Bill, with the cart—on foot, every day in the park, for the fun of it. Once he can read (or understand aurally) this small portion of the French text *without having further recourse to the English text,* he proceeds to the next few lines of bilingual reading or listening materials. As the student develops reading or listening skills, every other line of the *English* text is subsequently omitted. Such omissions become progressive until the student no longer has to depend on the English "crutch." The time required to reduce dependency on English to "asymptotic" zero will vary with the individual and in most cases will take years, not weeks or months.

Thus one might find in a reading selection the sentence

(22) *Jean a demandè à l'homme qui a été renversé par le camion de ne pas bouger.*

The student analyzes the sentence to determine "who asked who (that what knocked down) not to do what?" To do this, he observes that sentence 22 is really converted from two Frame *b* clauses such as:

S	P	C	C
$Act_{(tr)}$	Tr	DO	NO

(23) *Jean a demandé quelque chose à l'homme.*

(which has been converted to *Jean a demandé à l'homme quelque chose.*)

and

S	P	C
$Act_{(tr)}$	Tr	DO

(24) *Le camion a renversé l'homme*
plus one Frame *a* clause

S	P
$Act_{(In)}$	In

(25) *L'homme ne bouge pas*

The abstract interpretive rules, the details of which I shall omit here, help him to convert *le camion a renversé l'homme* into *qui a été renversé par le camion* and convert *l'homme ne bouge pas* into *de ne pas bouger* and then embed these two converted clauses in the proper slots to give sentence 22.

Furthermore any questions concerning newly introduced, i.e., heretofore unanalyzed, principles of grammatical or sound combinations would develop from the reading and listening materials themselves. They could be brought up for discussion by the students or by the teacher in class and be thoroughly "intellectualized" on the spot. This procedure makes the traditional "canned" review grammar obsolete, since the latter has little direct relevance to the structural principles contained in the reading or listening selection found in the average daily assignment.

An example of a "newly introduced" grammatical principle might go something like this. The student observes that the pronoun *en* is substituted for the embedded infinitival complement in sentence 26.

(26) Il parle *d'y aller*. → Il *en* parle.

However, in sentence 27, the pronoun *le* (not *en*) is substituted for what appears to be the same embedded construction.[23]

(27) Il déteste *d'y aller*. → Il *le* déteste.

Other embedded constructions might prove equally puzzling. For example, "*à* plus embedded infinitival complement" seems capable of being replaced by either *y* or *le*.

(28) Il a songé *à y aller*. → Il *y* a songé.
(29) Il a demandé *à y aller*. → Il *l'*a demandé.

Also consider the following sentences:

(30) Il nous a interdit *de le faire*. → Il nous *l'*a interdit.
(31) Il nous a empêchés *de le faire*. → Il nous *en* a empêchés.

In sentence 30 the past participle *interdit* is invariable. Therefore *nous* must be the indirect object and the past participle does not agree with it. The embedded infinitival complement *de le faire* functions as a direct object and is replaced by the pronoun *le*. In sentence

---

[23] For a perspicuous treatment of complementizers in embedded infinitive constructions, see Ronald W. Langacker, *A Transformational Syntax of French*, University of Illinois Ph.D. Dissertation, 1966, pp. 77-113.

31 the past participle *empêchés* agrees with *nous*. Therefore *nous* must be the (preceding) direct object and agrees with it. The embedded construction *de le faire* functions as NO (non-direct object) and is replaced by *en*. In other words, *de* of *de le faire* in sentence 31 functions as a preposition. But in sentence 30, *de* of *de le faire* does not have this function.

Similarly, *de* and *à* function as prepositions in sentences 26 and 28 respectively, but not in sentences 27 and 29. Then *de* and *à* in sentences 27, 29, and 30 appear to be "introducers" of the infinitival construction with no prepositional function. Following current practice, we shall refer to these introducers as "complementizers." When *de* and *à* serve as complementizers, the following infinitival construction functions as a direct object. In other words, since "*de* and *à* plus infinitival construction" have no prepositional function, then the embedded construction cannot be replaced by *en* or *y*.

Observe further that sentences 32 and 33 seem to be the same type of construction on the surface. They differ only as to the main verb (*ai conseillé, ai promis*).

(32) Je lui ai conseillé *d'y aller.* → Je *le* lui ai conseillé.
(33) Je lui ai promis *d'y aller.* → Je *le* lui ai promis.

In sentence 32 the "deleted" subject of the infinitive has the non-direct object *lui* (*à Jean*) as referent:

(J'ai conseillé quelque chose *à Jean;*
Jean y est allé.)

In sentence 33, however, the deleted subject of the infinitive has the subject of the main verb *J'* (*Je*) as referent:

(J'ai promis quelque chose à Jean;
J'y suis allé.)

Obviously, the reader (or listener) determines which of the two referents is the subject of the embedded infinitival construction because he knows the "inherent difference in meaning" between the verbs *conseiller* and *promettre.* Neither the concept of the "deleted subject of the infinitive" nor the principle of "preposition versus complementizer" is considered or even suspected in traditional pedagogical materials. Many "new grammatical principles" are constantly discovered during analysis of live reading and listening materials by both student and teacher.

Although we should continue to practice speaking (vocalizing) and writing (dictée, thème, version), far more emphasis should be placed on the acquisition of the listening and reading skills. By their very nature, "controlled" techniques with live materials allow for self-pacing and self-evaluation. By extending the learning period (*time-spread*) to allow for intellectualization and maturation, stress is placed on student achievement rather than on academic year blocks. In short, controlled materials take into consideration individual differences between students.

That passive skills must be developed before active skills is implicit even in the audiolingual "pedagogical pecking" order: listening, speaking, reading, and writing. However it is absolutely crucial to emphasize the passive skills: LISTENING, speaking, READING, writing. No real proficiency in a foreign language can be achieved in an artificial cultural environment until teachers, methodologists, and textbook writers recognize the importance of cognitive learning and the necessity for developing *mastery* in aural comprehension and reading.

As long as institutions of higher learning require graduate students in foreign language to accumulate credits designed to develop an appreciation of the culture of—rather than the skills in—the language, few students in high school or college are ever going to understand, speak, read, or write a foreign language.

CATHERINE A. MALEY*

The French Pronouns
of Direct Address

In French, where two pronouns of direct address are available, the form which one person chooses to address another reveals the social relationship between them. This social relationship can be described in non-linguistic terms vertically by class-status within a society, i.e., upper, middle, or lower class, or horizontally by age, sex, or urban or rural setting.

In order to determine the present-day usage of the pronouns of address in France, and to determine what differences, if any, exist in pronoun usage based on age, sex, setting, and social class, I undertook, in 1969, a study of the address patterns of the younger generation in France. To obtain the necessary information I devised a questionnaire, similar to the one used by Lambert (1967) in his study of the *tu–vous* usage in French Canada. Grade-school and high-school students were asked to complete the questionnaire which inquired about their use of *tu* and *vous* when speaking with persons who perform a service for them, with members of their family, with relatives, with friends, and also about the form of address others typically use when talking to them. It should be kept in mind that the data obtained in this study are only the reports of young people about one aspect of the roles they play in various social interactions,

---

* Romance Languages Department, University of North Carolina, Chapel Hill.

but not factual observations of the interaction. In particular, they do not include direct information from the other member of the interaction, i.e., the mother, the cousin, the teacher, etc.

Approximately 1600 male and female students completed the questionnaire. Students between the ages of 9 and 12 years are labeled as the elementary-school group, those between 13 and 19 are named the secondary-school group. I shall also refer to these two groups as "younger students" and "older students", or simply as "young" and "old" boys and girls. The responses of students younger than 9 years of age were not considered in the data analysis because of the unreliability of their answers, and their probable lack of understanding of the task put before them.

Testing was conducted in five cities in four different areas of France: Paris and its suburbs Montgeron and Sèvres; Reims (north central France); Molsheim (northeastern France); Cannes (southeastern France); and Cahors (southwestern France). The choice of these cities was determined only by the fact that I was able to obtain permission from friends or the school authorities in these cities to distribute my questionnaire in their schools.

Rural informants were designated on the basis of the father's occupation. There were 112 students whose fathers' occupations dealt with farming or related activities. Since only 6 of these students, 3 boys and 3 girls, were 12 years or younger, I cannot make any statistically valid urban-rural comparisons for the younger students.

Because no scales of social class standing in France were available, I enlisted the help and advice of a former sociology assistant in the Human Sciences department of the *Hautes Etudes Commerciales* (in Paris) in classifying the occupations of the children's fathers into the three social class groups, upper, middle, and lower. Accordingly, the children are put into the same three classes.

All questionnaires returned were used, excepting those where no report of the father's occupation was given, where the father was reported as dead, where the writing was illegible, or where the student's native language was not French.

The procedure for analysis was as follows. Comparisons of address patterns were made among six groups of informants, namely, two age levels (young-old), two setting samples (urban-rural), and the two sex groups. In order to find any variations in usage attributable to age differences, contrasts were made between younger and older boys and younger and older girls from both settings. Variations in usage based on setting were found by comparing urban and rural boys and urban and rural girls at the older age level only. Variations in the pronoun usage patterns attributable to sex were found by comparing boys and girls from both settings at both age levels. The two age groups and the two sex groups were then further divided into social classes to discover if any variations in the pattern of pronoun usage could be attributed to membership in a particular social class.

My discussion of the results obtained from the questionnaire will be based on the total and average percentages of *tu* and *vous* "sent" by each informant to a particular person, and of *tu* and *vous* "received" from a particular person by each informant. This exchange of the pronouns of address will be referred to as an interaction. The percentage data have been summarized on the basis of one table for each interaction, for example, informant and mother, informant and father, etc. Each table lists four groups: *young boy, old boy, young girl, old girl.* Under each of these four group headings will be found the total percentages of *tu* and *vous* sent and *tu* and *vous* received by young boys, young girls, old boys, old girls, in the urban and rural settings, and in the three social classes, upper, middle, and lower.

Since reciprocal *tu* is the pronoun usage established by all informants in their interactions with both close and distant family members, i.e., interactions with grandparents, parents, aunt, uncle, cousins, godfather, godmother, brother-in-law and sister-in-law, I will not include these tables in my discussion.

The results and discussion to follow explain and elaborate on the percentage results presented for each interaction in relationships outside the family. The following abbreviations will be used in the discussion of the average percentage results:

Y—young   O—old
B—boy   G—girl
TS—*tu* sent   TR—*tu* received
VS—*vous* sent   VR—*vous* received
E/O—either *tu* or *vous* sent or received
UC—upper class
MC—middle class
LC—lower class

INTERACTION WITH AN OLDER FEMALE ACQUAINTANCE WHO IS NOT A MEMBER OF THE FAMILY (Table 1)

The predominant pattern of address form with an older female acquaintance is non-reciprocal *tu—vous*. There are no marked urban-rural differences. A slight social class difference in the pattern is found with young boys: 72% of lower-class young boys send *tu,* 28% send *vous,* whereas the percentage of *tu* sent by the middle- and upper-class young boys is smaller:

middle class	62% send *tu*	36% send *vous*
upper class	57% send *tu*	43% send *vous.*

There are no social class differences for young girls. An average of 76% of young girls send *tu* (higher than the average of 64% for young boys), and 24% send *vous.* The percentage of *tu* sent by the old groups is less.

PERCENTAGE AVERAGE FIGURES
INTERACTION WITH AN OLDER FEMALE ACQUAINTANCE

	T S	V S	E/O	T R	V R	E/O
1. Y B	64	36		12	86	2
2. O B	51	46	3	9	89	2
3. Y G	76	24		14	80	6
4. O G	61	36	3	8	90	2

As the boys and girls approach their teens, the relationship with an older female acquaintance seems to be moving towards the reciprocal *vous* pattern, but is not yet completely established. Girls establish relatively more non-reciprocal *tu—vous* relations with older female acquaintances than do teen-age boys. The same is true of the young girls. Boys and girls, regardless of their age, are generally addressed with *vous* by older female acquaintances.

INTERACTION WITH AN OLDER MALE ACQUAINTANCE WHO IS NOT A MEMBER OF THE FAMILY (Table 2)

The predominant pattern of address form is to establish non-reciprocal *tu—vous* usage with an older male acquaintance. Rural and lower-class old boys tend to establish more non-reciprocal *tu—vous* relations with older male acquaintances than do urban and upper- and middle-class old boys. Old girls tend to establish fewer non-reciprocal *tu—vous* patterns with an older male acquaintance than do the old boys.

Old boys	T S	V S	E/O	T R	V R	E/O
1. U	59	40	1	13	84	2
2. R	75	25		15	85	
1. U C	57	40	3	15	81	4
2. M C	57	43		14	84	1
3. L C	70	29	1	12	87	1

The young boys and girls are more homogeneous in their usage of the non-reciprocal *tu–vous* pattern than their older counterparts. Social class does not affect the pronoun usage of the young groups.

PERCENTAGE AVERAGE FIGURES
INTERACTION WITH AN OLDER MALE ACQUAINTANCE

	T S	V S	E/O	T R	V R	E/O
1. Y B	71	29		10	88	2
2. O B	64	35	1	14	84	2
3. Y G	75	24	1	12	88	
4. O G	53	44	3	9	89	2

As with an older female acquaintance, teen-age boys and girls seem to be moving towards the reciprocal *vous* pattern with an older male acquaintance. Old boys establish relatively more non-reciprocal *tu* relations with older male acquaintances than do old girls. The pattern of pronoun address for young boys and girls in this interaction is similar. Regardless of age or social class, boys and girls are addressed with *vous* by an older male acquaintance.

INTERACTION WITH A BOY FRIEND OR A GIRL FRIEND (Tables 3, 4)

The predominant address form used when speaking to a friend, male or female, is reciprocal *tu* and over 90% of the informants in all groups use this form of interaction. There are no setting, sex, age, or social class variations in this interaction.

PERCENTAGE AVERAGE FIGURES
INTERACTION WITH A BOY FRIEND

	T S	V S	E/O	T R	V R	E/O
1. Y B	96	4		91	9	
2. O B	98	2		97	3	
3. Y G	98	2		91	9	
4. O G	98	2		97	3	

PERCENTAGE AVERAGE FIGURES
INTERACTION WITH A GIRL FRIEND

	T S	V S	E/O	T R	V R	E/O
1. Y B	95	5		89	11	
2. O B	98	2		97	3	
3. Y G	100			94	6	
4. O G	99	1		98	2	

INTERACTION WITH AN OLDER FEMALE STRANGER (Table 5)

The predominant mode of address for interaction between French children and an older female stranger is reciprocal *vous*. There are no setting differences. There is one significant age contrast, and that is between upper-class young girls and upper-class old girls. Upper-class young girls establish more non-reciprocal *tu* sent—*vous* received relations than do upper-class old girls. The middle- and lower-class old and young girls' pattern of address (i.e., reciprocal *vous*) is similar to that of the upper-class old girls.

SOCIAL CLASS PERCENTAGES
YOUNG AND OLD GIRLS

	T S	V S	E/O	T R	V R	E/O
1. Young girls						
a. U C	43	57		12	80	8
b. M C	26	73	1	9	90	1
c. L C	20	79	1	7	93	
2. Old girls						
a. U C	25	71	4	12	83	5
b. M C	25	74	1	13	84	3
c. L C	22	77	1	8	92	

PERCENTAGE AVERAGE FIGURES
INTERACTION WITH AN OLDER FEMALE STRANGER

	T S	V S	E/O	T R	V R	E/O
1. Y B	24	75	1	12	88	
2. O B	19	79	2	11	88	1
3. Y G	29	70	1	9	87	4
4. O G	25	73	2	11	86	3

INTERACTION WITH AN OLDER MALE STRANGER (Table 6)

The predominant mode of address for interaction between French children and an older male stranger is reciprocal *vous*. There are no significant urban-rural differences, nor are there any significant social class differences. A sex difference does exist; more girls, regardless of age, send *vous*, than do young or old boys.

PERCENTAGE AVERAGE FIGURES
INTERACTION WITH AN OLDER MALE STRANGER

	T S	V S	E/O	T R	V R	E/O
1. Y B	37	62	1	14	85	1
2. O B	33	66	1	16	83	1
3. Y G	27	72	1	9	87	4
4. O G	22	76	2	11	87	2

Apparently most children learn to withhold *tu* from all strangers, male and female, and expect to send and receive *vous*, regardless of age, sex, setting, or social class.

INTERACTION WITH A YOUNGER FEMALE STRANGER (Table 7)

At the young age level, both boys and girls establish reciprocal *tu* relations with younger female strangers, but the young boys have fewer reciprocal *tu* contacts than do the young girls:

	T S	V S	E/O	T R	V R	E/O
1. young boys	61	38	1	64	36	
2. young girls	75	24	1	76	23	1

No social class differences exist with the young girls' group. The lower-class young boys show a much higher percentage of reciprocal *tu* relations than do the middle- or upper-class young boys when they address a younger female stranger:

Young boys	T S	V S	E/O	T R	V R	E/O
1. U C	56	44		59	41	
2. M C	56	43	1	65	35	
3. L C	71	28	1	69	31	

Sixty-eight per cent of the old boys report receiving *tu* from a younger female stranger, regardless of setting or social class (31% receive *vous*, 1% either/or). The old boys are evenly divided as to the form they would use when addressing a younger female stranger; 51% send *tu*, 48% *vous*, 1% either/or. There is no marked change in usage from young middle- and upper-class boys to the old middle- and upper-class boys. There is, however, a considerable difference in usage between the young and old boys in the lower class:

Young boys	T S	V S	E/O	T R	V R	E/O
1. L C	71	28	1	69	31	
Old boys						
1. L C	50	50		66	34	

A similar situation exists for the old girls in *all* social classes. Only 42% of the old girls would send *tu* (as compared to 75% of the young girls), 58% *vous*. In return, 70% of the old girls would expect *tu* from a younger female stranger, 28% *vous*, 2% either/or. The old boys' and girls' pattern for the pronoun form received is the same. The popularity of the non-reciprocal *vous* sent—*tu* received form of address increases with age, particularly with older girls; teen-agers expect to receive *tu* from an unfamiliar younger child and to address him or her with *vous*.

There are no urban-rural differences, but, as the statistics quoted above show, young boys and girls tend to establish reciprocal *tu* relations with a younger female stranger (the young girls more so than the young boys, probably because they are addressing a member of their own sex). In contrast, the tendency with the old boys and girls is to establish non-reciprocal *vous–tu* relations, and the old girls send more *vous* than the old boys (58% for girls, 48% for boys).[1] The majority of old boys and girls expect to receive *tu* from a younger female stranger, boys 68%, girls 70%.

PERCENTAGE AVERAGE FIGURES
INTERACTION WITH A YOUNGER FEMALE STRANGER

	T S	V S	E/O	T R	V R	E/O
1. Y B	61	38	1	64	36	
2. O B	51	48	1	68	31	1
3. Y G	75	24	1	76	23	1
4. O G	42	58		70	28	2

INTERACTION WITH A YOUNGER MALE STRANGER (Table 8)

At the young age level, both boys and girls establish reciprocal *tu* relations with a younger male stranger:

	T S	V S	E/O	T R	V R	E/O
1. Y B	67	33		69	31	
2. Y G	69	30	1	76	24	

More young girls than young boys use *tu* with a younger *female* stranger. With a younger *male* stranger both young boys and girls send *tu*. A slight difference in the form received from a younger male stranger does exist in that 7% more girls than boys expect to receive *tu*. There are no significant social class differences within the young girls' group or the young boys' group, but the lower-class boys and girls show a higher percentage of reciprocal *tu* relations than do the upper- or middle-class boys and girls:

---

[1] This difference may be due to the old girls modeling themselves on an adult female role; 87% of the old and young girls' groups expect to receive *vous* from an older female stranger.

	T S	V S	E/O	T R	V R	E/O
Young boys						
1. U C	63	37		63	37	
2. M C	62	37	1	69	31	
3. L C	74	25	1	75	25	
Young girls						
1. U C	61	35	4	84	16	
2. M C	70	30		74	24	1
3. L C	75	25		69	31	

Seventy-five per cent of the old boys report receiving *tu* from a younger male stranger (regardless of setting or social class), 24% receive *vous*, and 1% one or the other. Sixty per cent of the old boys send *tu*, 39% *vous*. There is no marked change in usage from the upper- and middle-class young boys to their older counterparts in the upper and middle classes, but the percentage of *tu* sent by lower-class young boys is much higher than the percentage of *tu* sent by lower-class old boys:

	T S	V S	E/O	T R	V R	E/O
Lower class						
1. Y B	74	25	1	75	25	
2. O B	58	42		74	26	

Sixty-seven per cent of the old girls report receiving *tu* from a younger male stranger, regardless of setting or social class; 31% receive *vous*, 2% one or the other. Only 39% of the old girls send *tu* to a younger male stranger (versus 60% of the old boys); 60% send *vous*, 1% one or the other. No appreciable urban-rural or social class differences exist within the old girls' group.

Therefore, the tendency for young and old boys and young girls is to establish reciprocal *tu* relations with a younger male stranger. But the predominant tendency for old girls is to establish non-reciprocal *vous* sent—*tu* received relations.

PERCENTAGE AVERAGE FIGURES
INTERACTION WITH A YOUNGER MALE STRANGER

	T S	V S	E/O	T R	V R	E/O
1. Y B	67	33		69	31	
2. O B	60	39	1	75	24	1
3. Y G	69	30	1	76	24	
4. O G	39	60	1	67	31	2

INTERACTION WITH A CLASSROOM TEACHER (Table 9)

The overwhelming majority of students, regardless of age, sex, setting, or social class, receive *vous* from their classroom teacher.

PERCENTAGE AVERAGE FIGURES
INTERACTION WITH A CLASSROOM TEACHER

	T S	V S	E/O	T R	V R	E/O
1. Y B	59	36	5	6	94	
2. O B	15	83	2	3	96	1
3. Y G	61	34	5	8	92	
4. O G	3	95	2	1	99	

As one might expect, students (both girls and boys) at the secondary level use *vous* to address their teacher, thus *vous* used reciprocally is the predominant pronoun of address used by students and their teacher at the secondary level. There are no setting differences in the old male and female groups. No social class distinctions exist in the old girls' group. Slight social class distinctions appear in the old boys' group:

Old boys	T S	V S	E/O	T R	V R	E/O
1. U C	15	82	3	3	93	4
2. M C	9	88	3	3	97	
3. L C	21	77	2	2	95	3

Notice that when compared with the lower and upper classes, the middle-class old boys use *tu* less when they address a classroom teacher. The majority of old boys, regardless of social class, report receiving *vous* from their classroom teacher.

The predominant pattern at the elementary age level is non-reciprocal *tu* sent—*vous* received relations with the classroom teacher. The lower-class young boys tend more toward non-reciprocal *tu*—*vous* relations than do the upper- and middle-class young boys.

Young boys	T S	V S	E/O	T R	V R	E/O
1. U C	50	46	4	4	96	
2. M C	57	36	7	7	93	
3. L C	69	24	7	7	92	1

Middle-class young girls tend to establish more non-reciprocal *tu*—*vous* relations than middle-class young boys.

Young girls	T S	V S	E/O	T R	V R	E/O
1. U C	51	45	4	6	94	
2. M C	72	22	6	5	94	1
3. L C	60	34	6	13	87	

The percentage figures for upper-class young girls and upper-class young boys are approximately the same. Lower-class young boys tend more toward non-reciprocal *tu–vous* relations than do the lower-class young girls.

INTERACTION WITH A PHYSICAL-EDUCATION TEACHER (Table 10)

The pattern of address for this special type of teacher, whose relations with students are less academic, is different from the pattern of address used with the classroom teacher, in that more reciprocal *tu* relations are established at both age levels.

The predominant form of address received by all students from their physical-education teacher, regardless of age, setting, sex, or social class is *vous*.

PERCENTAGE AVERAGE FIGURES
INTERACTION WITH A PHYSICAL-EDUCATION TEACHER

	T S	V S	E/O	T R	V R	E/O
1. Y B	85	14	1	11	89	
2. O B	58	42		6	94	
3. Y G	79	19	2	7	93	
4. O G	21	79		2	98	

At the elementary level, the predominant form of address used by both male and female students to address their physical-education teacher is *tu*. Differences in percentages of usage by social class are not significant.

The old male and female students substantially reduce the amount of *tu* when they address their physical-education teacher. There is a significant shift in usage when one moves from the young age group to the old age group: in the male group the percentage of *tu* sent is reduced from 85% to 58%; in the female group the reduction is even more marked, from 79% to 21%.

There are no significant urban-rural or class differences in the old male and female groups of informants.

INTERACTION WITH A MONITEUR (OR MONITRICE) DE SPORTS (Table 11)

In France, a *moniteur* or *monitrice de sports* is an assistant to the physical-education teacher. Normally, this person would be the same sex as the students, thus a *moniteur* would help with the training of boys and a *monitrice* with the training of girls.

The predominant form of address received by all students from a *moniteur* or *monitrice*, regardless of age, setting, sex, or social class, is *vous*.

At the young age level, the most predominant form used by male and female students when they address their *moniteur* or *monitrice* is *tu*, hence the established pattern is non-reciprocal *tu–vous* in the interaction of the young informants and their *moniteur* or *monitrice*. There are no social class differences as regards the usage of *tu* by the young girls' group. However, marked social class differences exist in the percentage of *tu* used by young males to address their *moniteur:*

Young boys	T S	V S	E/O	T R	V R	E/O
1. U C	64	36		18	82	
2. M C	85	14	1	22	78	
3. L C	96	4		23	77	

Notice that the largest percentage of *tu* sent is found in the lower-class group of young boys. The middle-class and lower-class boys are more homogeneous in their usage of *tu* to address their *moniteur* in contrast to the smaller percentage of *tu* sent by the upper-class young boys.

There are important sex and age differences that modify the *tu–vous* usage in the teen-age group. Only 66% of the old boys send *tu*, 34% *vous*. Old girls show more of a reduction in the usage of *tu* with their *monitrice* than do the old boys; 41% send *tu*, 58% send *vous*.

No appreciable urban-rural or social class differences exist in the pronoun usage of the old boys. Old urban girls, however, use *tu* with their *monitrice* 46%, *vous* 53%, whereas the old rural girls report they use *tu* 24% and *vous* 76%. Fifty-nine per cent of the upper-class old girls send *tu*, 38% send *vous*. The middle- and lower-class old girls tend to use less *tu* sent than do the upper-class old girls: in the middle class 40% send *tu*, 59% send *vous;* in the lower class 38% of the old girls send *tu*, 62% send *vous*.

AVERAGE PERCENTAGE FIGURES
INTERACTION WITH A MONITEUR OR MONITRICE DE SPORTS

	T S	V S	E/O	T R	V R	E/O
1. Y B	82	18		21	79	
2. O B	66	34		18	81	1
3. Y G	82	15	3	15	80	5
4. O G	41	58	1	11	85	4

INTERACTION WITH MALE SERVICE PERSONNEL (Table 12)

There are many different norms for interacting with male service personnel, such as a bus driver or a sales clerk, and these appear to be influenced by setting, age, sex, and social class factors. At the elementary age level, the predominant address form is the non-reciprocal *tu* sent—*vous* received, but the predominance varies within the social class.

Young boys	T S	V S	E/O	T R	V R	E/O
1. U C	50	50		12	88	
2. M C	67	33		13	86	1
3. L C	72	28		18	81	1
Young girls	T S	V S	E/O	T R	V R	E/O
1. U C	63	35	2	11	87	2
2. M C	58	42		9	90	1
3. L C	83	17		12	88	

The largest majority of informants who send *tu* are the lower-class young boys and young girls. There is no great difference in usage between the upper-class and middle-class young girls. The percentage of *tu* sent by the middle- and lower-class young boys is higher than the percentage of *tu* sent by the upper-class young boys when they address male service personnel.

All groups noticeably change their mode of interaction with male service personnel when they enter into the old age groups, with the exception of the old rural boys, who maintain the non-reciprocal *tu—vous* pattern, and become, at the teen-age level, quite distinct, their norm being significantly different from both that of the old urban boys and the old rural and urban girls:

	T S	V S	E/O	T R	V R	E/O
1. Old rural boys	82	17	1	22	77	1
2. Old urban boys	43	57		12	86	2
3. Old rural girls	26	74		6	94	
4. Old urban girls	18	81	1	3	96	1

The change in address for urban boys from the non-reciprocal *tu—vous* relations to a more reciprocal *vous* relationship with male service personnel reflects the change in age. Both rural and urban girls report a greater use of reciprocal *vous* at the old age level. There is not as sharp a reduction in the use of *tu* in the old boys' group as in the old girls' group.

AVERAGE PERCENTAGE FIGURES
INTERACTION WITH MALE SERVICE PERSONNEL

	T S	V S	E/O	T R	V R	E/O
1. Y B	63	37		14	85	1
2. O B	53	47		13	85	2
3. Y G	68	32		11	88	1
4. O G	20	80		3	95	2

Social class differences are more clearly marked in the young and old male groups than in the young and old female groups:

Old boys	T S	V S	E/O	T R	V R	E/O
1. U C	31	67	1	8	88	4
2. M C	43	57		13	87	
3. L C	65	35		18	81	1

Old girls	T S	V S	E/O	T R	V R	E/O
1. U C	8	90	2	5	92	3
2. M C	19	80	1	3	97	
3. L C	25	75		2	97	1

The lower class, regardless of age, establishes more non-reciprocal *tu–vous* relationships with male service personnel than do the middle and upper classes. No appreciable differences based on sex are found in the young groups, but there are definite differences in usage based on sex in the old groups. Old boys send *tu* more than old girls (50% versus 20%). Age is an important factor in the reduction of *tu* sent, because the old groups, male and female, tend to use *tu* less with male service personnel and are moving to a reciprocal *vous* usage. Upper-class children of all groups (male, female, young, old) send *tu* substantially less than do middle- and lower-class children of all groups. This may mean that upper-class children learn to keep their distance from male service personnel by using *vous* to address them.

INTERACTION WITH FEMALE SERVICE PERSONNEL (Table 13)

The norms of pronoun usage with a maid, a concierge, or other female service personnel are substantially the same as those employed for male service personnel.

AVERAGE PERCENTAGE FIGURES
INTERACTION WITH FEMALE SERVICE PERSONNEL

	T S	V S	E/O	T R	V R	E/O
1. Y B	57	42	1	18	81	1
2. O B	48	51	1	12	86	2
3. Y G	68	26	6	18	78	4
4. O G	36	63	1	7	91	2

The predominant address pattern with the young male and female groups when they address female service personnel is non-reciprocal *tu* sent—*vous* received. There are no significant social class differences in the young group of informants, except for a slight difference in usage between upper-class young boys and upper-class young girls: 43% of the former and 63% of the latter use *tu*.

The old male and female informants tend to use *tu* less with female service personnel, and are moving to a reciprocal *vous* usage. A distinct urban-rural difference exists in the old boys' group:

	T S	V S	E/O
1. Old urban boys	40	59	1
2. Old rural boys	72	28	

The urban-rural difference is not as marked with the old girls:

	T S	V S	E/O
1. Old urban girls	32	68	1
2. Old rural girls	49	51	

Notice that old rural boys use *tu* to address female service personnel more than do the old rural girls. The same is true of lower-class young boys who report using *tu* to address female service personnel 67%, whereas only 43% of the lower-class old girls use *tu*.

Old boys	T S	V S	E/O	T R	V R	E/O
1. U C	25	72	3	11	85	4
2. M C	37	63		13	87	
3. L C	67	33		14	86	

The percentage of *tu* sent and *vous* sent by the upper- and middle-class old boys and girls does not vary widely.

INTERACTION WITH EMPLOYER (Table 14)

Less than one-half of the male and female students who completed the questionnaire answered the question concerning the interaction with an employer, indicating, perhaps, that part-time employment for children is not common in France.

Only 134 young boys and girls replied to this question. The predominant address pattern of those who did answer was to establish a non-reciprocal *tu—vous* usage with an employer:

	T S	V S	E/O	T R	V R	E/O
1. Y B	56	40	4	14	86	
2. Y G	65	29	6	10	90	

There was a variation in social classes in the amount of *tu* sent with the young boys: the middle- and upper-class young boys' percentages are more similar (upper — 38% send *tu*, 50% *vous*, 12% either one or the other; middle — 48% send *tu*, 52% *vous*) when compared with the lower-class young boys who send *tu* 80% and *vous* 20% to address an employer. As for young girls, the upper- and lower-class percentages are the same (71%, 70%, respectively, send *tu*), but the middle-class percentage is much lower (43% send *tu*).

There is a significant shift in usage from the young girls' group to the old girls' group where the predominant form of address with an employer is reciprocal *vous*: 84% of the old girls address an employer with *vous*, 16% with *tu* (versus young girls who send *tu* 65%, *vous* 29%). There are no significant urban-rural or social class distinctions in the old girls' group.

The percentages of *tu* sent in the old boys' group are less than the percentages of *tu* sent by the young boys' group; the sharpest reduction in percentage is seen in the lower-class boys' group:

Old boys	T S	V S	E/O	T R	V R	E/O
1. U C	23	77		3	97	
2. M C	31	69		9	91	
3. L C	51	49		10	90	

There is also a marked urban-rural difference in the old boys' group:

	T S	V S	E/O	T R	V R	E/O
1. Old urban boys	35	65		3	97	
2. Old rural boys	59	41		10	90	

Old rural boys report sending *tu* to an employer 24% more than old urban boys.

The old girls show a tendency to establish more reciprocal *vous* relations with an employer than the old boys (84% versus 60%).

AVERAGE PERCENTAGE FIGURES
INTERACTION WITH AN EMPLOYER

	T S	*V S*	*E/O*	*T R*	*V R*	*E/O*
1. Y B	55	41	4	12	88	
2. O B	40	60		9	91	
3. Y G	61	35	4	16	84	
4. O G	16	84		4	96	

What are the implications of this study for the native speaker of English learning French? Since English no longer makes a distinction between the familiar *thou* and the formal *you* pronouns of address, these distinctions in usage have to be taught. Most American textbooks for teaching French contain a short statement to the effect that *tu* is used to address members of a family, friends, children, and pets. A general statement of this type is hardly sufficient for teaching the *tu—vous* usage.

The questionnaire results show that reciprocal *tu* is the common pattern of pronoun usage between members of a family, between close and distant relatives, and between friends. However, it is very difficult to establish set rules for the *tu—vous* usage outside the circle of family and friends because the choice of the pronoun of address becomes complex and may have very different shades of meaning depending upon the context of the interaction, and the sex, age, and personality of the speakers. Membership in a particular social class no longer seems to dictate the choice of either *tu* or *vous*.

The following statements, based on the questionnaire results, can, therefore, be used as guidelines in teaching the *tu—vous* usage outside the circle of family or friends to students of French. They should not, of course, be considered as rules, but only indications of usage as reported by the informants.

As one might expect from the age group of the informants, the non-reciprocal *vous* sent—*tu* received form is rarely used in the interaction of an informant and another person.

All informants report non-reciprocal *tu* sent—*vous* received in their interactions with an older female acquaintance or an older male acquaintance, but the percentage of *tu* sent lessens as boys and girls approach their teens and the relationship seems to move towards the reciprocal *vous* pattern.

Reciprocal *tu* is reported as the predominant address pattern in all informants' interactions with a younger male or a younger female stranger. Contrary to the observations on usage as stated in most textbooks (i.e., address children with *tu*), all groups of informants report that reciprocal *vous* is the predominant address pattern used in their interactions with an older male or an older female stranger. All informants regardless of age, report being addressed with *vous* by their teachers. The young informants report using *tu* to address their teachers, while the old informants report using *vous* to address their teachers. It must be remembered that since a French child has spent his pre-school days in the family milieu, he is accustomed to the reciprocal *tu* form of address when speaking with adults. Thus, he must learn that adults outside the family circle will address him with *vous*. This probably accounts for the fact that at the elementary school level, a teacher uses *vous* to address a student, rather than *tu*. By the time a child has left the elementary school and entered the lycée, the predominant pattern of address between a student and a teacher is reciprocal *vous*.

It is evident that the *tutoiement* based on familiarity has considerably increased in the twentieth century. Jean Dubois, a French psychologist, comments in his book, *Les Cadres dans la société de consommation*, on the influence of the clubs, vacation centers, and similar organizations in breaking down class barriers and facilitating a greater degree of intimacy between people, an intimacy which finds vocal expression in *tutoiement*: "Le loisir n'est plus le temps de la famille, même élargie, il devient le temps de la tribu, le temps des clubs. Tous ceux qui sont allés au 'club' attestent de son efficacité à réaliser un étonnant mélange social, à supprimer toutes les barrières, y compris—se plaignent les moralistes—celle entre les sexes. Le jeu veut qu'on puisse prénommer, tutoyer n'importe qui."[2]

The answers to the questionnaire show that the younger generation has come to regard as familiar or intimate many personal relations that their elders would have considered distant or formal, and they accordingly are more liberal in their use of *tutoiement*. This is true in particular if the speakers are of the same age, or the same sex, or both, or if there exists between them a certain affinity, since they are fellow workers, fellow students, or members of an organization that unites like-minded persons such as a club, a political party, a professional society, or a religious community.

What is the meaning of the increase of *tutoiement* among the younger generation examined in this study? Does their use of *tu* reflect a wider change of pronominal usage among French people? Does it portend such a change, a change that is to go into effect

2 Jean Dubois, "Les Cadres dans la société de consommation" (Paris, 1969), p. 128.

when their generation reaches adulthood? Or should one assume that the youngsters, now using *tu* with exuberance, will adopt the ways of their elders as soon as they grow up? In other words, is this generation gap in forms of address a passing phenomenon, or will the present ways of the young eventually harden into general custom? Of course, no sure answer can be given. Still, one may perhaps assume that the young will not completely give up their habits, and that *tutoiement* will in coming generations be more common than it is now.

ROBERT A. MORREY*

The Sequential Drilling Method: An Organizing Concept for Classroom Drills

By 1960 most theorists in foreign-language education were advocating a method of teaching which became known as the "audiolingual" approach.[1] The advocates of this audiolingual method made one extremely important contribution to the field of foreign-language teaching: they reintroduced the spoken language into the ordinary classroom through their "pattern drills". Since the introduction of pattern drills, a number of writers such as Brooks, Lado, Huebener, Oliva, Politzer have specified a large number of different types of drills which can be used. Rivers has gone so far as to describe the characteristics of good pattern drills (Rivers, *Teaching Foreign-Language Skills*, 1968, pp. 103-105). However, none of the writers has considered in detail what the order of presentation of these different drills should be. Are there some organizing principles which can be followed which would indicate what kinds of drills are better suited for initial drills work? What kinds of sequencing of drills lead to the most efficient learning of new material?

General answers to these questions have been supplied in the

* Foreign Language Education Specialist, College of Notre Dame, Belmont, California.
[1] The data and results desribed in this article are based on the dissertation study "The Effects of Sequential Oral Drilling with Second Conjugation French Verbs upon Student Performance" submitted by the author to Stanford University in August, 1970.

statements of a few writers. For example, Politzer has stated in a description of the drilling pattern of a teacher that "he [the teacher] proceeded from a very strict amount of control (repetition) to a gradual withdrawal of control (substitution and transformation) to a point where he actually allowed the student to produce his own sentences without any immediately preceding cue" (Politzer, "The Effective Use of the Structure Drill", 1965, p. 678). Later, Politzer describes in general terms how oral drills could be organized. "It [pattern practice] must, of course, *start* with the repetition type of exercise. . . . Then, however, the pattern can be practiced through substitution in the model sentence. The next step may involve an exercise in which the pattern is derived from the transformation of another similar pattern or serves as the basis for such transformation. Then the basic pattern may be expanded into a somewhat larger one. Since the ultimate goal is the use of the pattern in actual conversation, the final step in pattern practice should be the use of the pattern in response to a 'conversational' cue which is completely dissimilar to the pattern itself. . . ." (Politzer, *Performance Criteria for the Foreign Language Teacher*, 1967, p. 16). The most precise statement concerning the organization of oral drills was made by Rivers in her description of "stages of presentation" of drills. She indicates that "As the drill period begins, he [the student] is presented aurally with several examples of the pattern grouped together in a repetition drill. . . . At the next stage, the student is asked to reproduce the pattern with some difference in lexical content in response to a cue. . . . When the teacher judges by the alert and ready response of the class that the pattern has been assimilated, he will engage the students in a mixed drill, or a multiple-substitution drill, to see whether the response is still prompt and accurate. . . . He [the teacher] will not, however, consider the pattern to be thoroughly learned until he sees that the students are able to use it in the wider context of conversation interchanges in the classroom" (Rivers, 1968, pp. 106-107).

Writers in the area of English as a Second Language also recognize the problem. In discussions of college-level instruction, Clifford Prator describes what he feels is a dichotomy between pure language classes and literaturec lasses. He says that while the language classes stress habit formation or manipulative activities, the literature classes which occur later in the program emphasize almost exclusively "activities designed . . . to encourage the free communication of thought" and no "gradual and orderly transition" is made from the one type of activity to the other (Prator, "Development of a Manipulation-

Communication Scale", 1964, p. 57). He goes on to advocate that there should be a "very gradual shift from manipulation. [Prator's term for strictly controlled pattern drills] to communication which is accomplished through progressive decontrol" (Prator, "Development...", 1964, pp. 59-60).

Prator has not gone much further than to advocate a gradual transition from one kind of activity to another; he has given very little indication—only a few examples—of how to determine what drills and activities should occur at what time. In comparison to Prator, Paulston in a very recent article "Structural Pattern Drills: A Classification" sets forth certain general principles for determining what pattern drills should be presented early and which ones later in the drill sequence. She defines three basic types of drills—mechanical, meaningful, communicative—by analyzing them in terms of "(1) expected terminal behavior, (2) of response control, (3) of the type of learning process involved and (4) of utterance response" (Paulston, "Structural . . .", 1970, p. 189). She defines a mechanical drill as one "where there is complete control of the response, where there is only one correct way of responding." She goes on to say that "The expected terminal behavior of such drills is the automatic use of manipulative patterns and is commensurate with the assumption that language learning is habit formation" (p. 189). She goes on to define meaningful drills as ones where "there is still control of the response (although it may be correctly expressed in more than one way and as such is less suitable for choral drilling), but the student cannot complete the drill without fully understanding structurally and semantically what he is saying" (p. 190). Finally she states that "In a communicative drill there is no control on the response. The student has free choice of answer, and the criterion of selection here is his own opinion of the real world—whatever he wants to say. Whatever control there is lies in the stimulus" (p. 191).

Paulston advocates that same transition from manipulative or mechanical to communicative activities as does Prator. Paulston also recognizes the need for some classification of structural drills according to an organizing principle such as the one she proposes, but neither Paulston or Prator actually provides us with a usable classification of the great variety of oral drills; that job is left up to the teacher who rarely has the time for such activities.

However, in an independently prepared article, I have provided a five-level classification of oral drills which is based upon movement from mechanical to communicative activities. Two other principles for classifying drills are also implicit in the classification: namely, the length of the cue or what Paulston refers to in her article as the "amount range" and the increasing dissimilarity between the cue and the response of a student. Thus, according to the first principle, any drill can be made more complex by lengthening the amount of material that the student has to remember in order to produce an answer.

The second principle is similar to what Paulston labels as the "restructuring range," that is "the type of restructuring of a cue and the complexity of this restructuring which a learner must go through to arrive at a response" (Paulston, p. 188). It has been defined in greater detail by Robert Politzer in his article "Toward Psycholinguistic Models of Language Instruction" as a procedure through which cues are made increasingly dissimilar from expected responses as the drill progresses (Politzer, "Models . . ." p. 154). As an example of the dissimilarity principle, repetition drills would be the easiest kind of drill since the student is expected to repeat exactly what the teacher said; open questions such as—what will you do this afternoon?—are the most difficult because the student has to formulate the complete answer.

Paulston feels that "The major drawback with these typologies [amount range and restructuring range] is that they do not provide a method of gradation of drills" (p. 188); nevertheless, I have attempted to define the following five levels of drills using these principles: Repetition, Basic production, Short sentence, Advanced drills, and Free conversation. A teacher following this method would begin by explaining the concept to be learned. Then actual drilling is begun, and the teacher uses a number of drills organized according to the principles mentioned above. In the first two levels, the drills are very mechanical and also short. They are specifically designed to deal with phrases and small blocks of material, not with complete sentences, and the purpose of such drills is to *begin* to establish automatic habits—these drills are not, however, worked over so long that the students cease to be "challenged" by them. The third level, *Short sentence drills*, moves into the realm of meaningful drills since they are based on short sentences. In the last two levels, the cues for drills become longer, the drills are based more and more on meaningful and communicative activities with cues becoming more dissimilar from the expected responses. This model thus provides an organizing framework for a large number of different drills which are also classified into the different levels so that language teachers have a clear picture of what drills to use and when to use them (Morrey, "Successive Degrees of Oral Drilling . . .").

In order to verify that this method of drilling—which is called the Sequential Drilling Method (SDM)—is indeed an efficient method of structuring drill work, a study was conducted to determine how variation in student achievement at the high-school level was related to different sequences of drills. Obviously, if one wants to compare student achievement with drilling practices of the teacher, some manner of observing the teacher is necessary; a systematic observation instrument was called for. Unfortunately, most of the work done with observation scales in the past was done in the affective domain, and these scales were not applicable to observing skill activities. However, through use of the techniques and procedures developed for work in the affective domain, a special scale—the Sequential Drilling Observation Scale (SDOS)—was developed. With this instrument, a trained observer records each cue in an oral drill session on a special observation sheet. Following the drill session, a summary sheet is prepared which indicates the number and kind of oral drills done during each minute of the drilling session. This is the teacher's drilling profile, and it clearly shows whether teachers start with repetition drills and gradually move to short sentence and then longer drills, whether they use only drills at one level (i.e., mechanical drills to the exclusion of all other types), or whether they begin with sentences and gradually move to basic production and repetition drills. In addition to the drilling profile, a procedure for numerically quantifying the profile was developed. The resulting numerical score was designed to provide an easily interpretable statement as to whether or not a teacher's drilling pattern was close to the model described in the Sequential Drilling Method. Since a higher SDOS score indicates a drilling pattern more closely approximating the SDM pattern, it was then possible to look at the numerical score for a teacher and have a rather good idea whether or not the teacher conducted oral drills according to the SDM. With a detailed description of the drilling method and an instrument for observing teachers' drilling practices, it became possible to examine the effects of sequencing oral drills on student achievement.

HYPOTHESIS

In formal terms, this experiment was undertaken to determine if the students of teachers who follow the Sequential Drilling Method perform better on two proficiency tests of French -ir verbs than similar students of teachers who follow the SDM less closely when prior ability and aptitude is statistically controlled.

SAMPLE

The teachers and classes in this study were chosen from five large school districts located within 30 miles of Palo Alto, California. The general population included farm and factory workers and professional persons.

The study attempted to work with "typical" first-year French classes. Two main criteria were used in selecting classes: that they be "first-year" French classes and that the basic text for the class be the *A-LM French Level One* textbook (first edition). The final sample consisted of 304 students and 17 teachers. Of the 17 classes, two were composed of students who had studied two years of French in the junior high school before entering first-year French in the high school. In the other 15 classes, the percentage of students with two years of French before entering high school ranged from zero to about 10.

DESIGN OF THE STUDY

Seventeen first-year classes and the seventeen teachers formed the experimental sample. The classes were initially tested for foreign-language aptitude using the Modern Language Aptitude Test (MLAT) and on knowledge of and ability to use -er verb forms. These initial tests took place after the classes had completed three months of regular instruction. At this point, each teacher received a five-page pamphlet detailing the material to be taught and stating what the students were to do in the criterion tests: the behavioral objectives. Each teacher next proceeded to teach the same three -ir verbs to his class for 20 minutes on each of two successive days; these lessons were tape recorded. On the day following the second of the two lessons, the Ir Written criterion test and the Ir Oral criterion test were administered. The Ir Oral test was administered individually to a randomly selected sample of each class and not to every student in the class.

Subsequent analysis of the audio-tapes allowed the experimenter to assign to each teacher an SDOS score which indicated how closely that teacher's oral drilling method corresponded to the SDM. As stated earlier, the SDOS score is simply a numerical figure, computed from the SDOS profile sheets, which reflects the degree to which a teacher's oral drilling method approximates the Sequential Drilling Method (SDM).

Since these SDOS scores were crucial to the later analysis, it was important to examine them for validity and reliability. Validity was in this case not difficult to establish. We stated at the outset that we wished to determine the number and sequence of the drills the teacher used in the classroom, and the profiles obtained during the recording process did indicate exactly what the sequence of drills was and how many times drills were repeated. Hence, the instrument can be said to have *face validity*. In reference to reliability, a comparison of scores for two observers (interrater reliability) was not attempted because all the scoring was done by one person. However, a 97-99 percent agreement was obtained between a first SDOS score and one computed independently six weeks later by the same observer from an audio-recording of the original lesson; this data indicates that the observer was consistent in his scoring procedure over a period of time. Another type of reliability was obtained by comparing drilling profiles for the same teacher teaching the same lesson but to different classes [a few teachers wanted to teach the experimental lessons to their other first-year classes as well as to the class in the study, and it was thus possible in these cases to obtain more than one teacher-score for the same lesson]. Again, a 90-99 percent agreement was found. According to this information concerning the reliability of the SDOS instrument, it is clear that a well-trained observer can provide a reliable recording of a teacher's drilling procedure.

In addition to the SDOS score already discussed, measures on other variables were obtained from the Modern Language Aptitude Test, an Er test, and two criterion tests—the Ir Written test and the Ir Oral test. The Modern Language Aptitude Test (MLAT) is, of course, a well-known and carefully prepared test for measuring a student's aptitude for learning a foreign language. The other three tests—the Er test, the Ir Written and the Ir Oral—were designed and administered by the experimenter, and the structure and vocabulary used in each test were strictly limited to material with which the students were familiar.

The Er test was used as a pretest to measure a basic level of achievement in and ability to use regular -er French verbs. The material covered by this test was taught by the regular teachers prior to the beginning of the study. The test itself consisted of three fifteen-item sections, the first of which was concerned with listening comprehension. In the first part of this section, the students listened to five general questions in French, i.e., *A quelle heure déjeunez-vous à l'école?* The students were required to write an answer either in French or in English. The second part of this first section consisted of ten items. For these items, the students listened to a cue presented on tape and then selected the correct response from three choices provided. All of the ten items were of the following pattern: the students heard a subject pronoun, *nous*, and then three verb forms, *joue, jouons, jouez*. The three verb forms were also printed on the answer sheets and the students just circled the correct form.

The second section of the Er test was designed to test sound/symbol correspondence and recognition of correct -er verb forms. In the first part of this section, students listened to a subject pronoun-verb form unit spoken on tape, i.e., *ils aiment*, and then chose its correct written representation on the answer sheet from these four answers: *ils aimaient, il aime, ils aiment, il aima*. In the next part of this section, the students were given a written cue, i.e., *tu vas*, in which one letter was underlined. They were to compare the sound represented by that letter with the sounds of similarly underlined letters in four possible responses: *ma sœur, j'ai, vais, beau*. The students would then circle the answer in which the underlined letters sounded the same as the underlined letter in the cue, i.e., *ma sœur*.

In the third and final section of the Er test, the students were requested to actually write down correct verb forms when given sentences in which the verb was in its infinitive form: *Je (écouter) la radio*. They were also presented with sentences in which the words were scrambled with the verb in the infinitive and were asked to create a sentence. For instance, one such sentence was: *loin d'ici, habiter, nous*, which the students were supposed to rewrite as: *nous habitons loin d'ici*. The final five questions were simply translation items from French to English.

The Ir Written test was composed of two sections modelled after sections I and III in the Er test but using -ir verbs. The Ir Oral test was an oral production test for which a random sample of students from each class was requested to respond individually to a set of tape-recorded cues. This test consisted of twelve items. In the first ten items, the student was given a verb infinitive and a subject pronoun: *chercher—je*. The student was then asked to respond orally with the subject pronoun and then the correct verb form: *je cherche*. The last two items were short French questions which the students were supposed to answer orally, i.e., *Qu'est-ce que vous choisissez pour le déjeuner, vous et Pierre?* The responses of each student were recorded, and both pronunciation and grammatical correctness were considered in determining the students' score.

Intraclass reliability coefficients were computed for each subtest of the Er and Ir Written tests and these are given herewith in Tables

1 and 2 along with intercorrelation coefficients. The reliability of the Ir Oral test was found to be .71 for the twelve item test.

TABLE 1   INTERCORRELATION OF SUBTESTS OF THE ER PRETEST

| | | Intercorrelation | | Correlation |
	I	II	III	with total
Subtest 1	(.60)			.74
Subtest II	.53	(.74)		.89
Subtest III	.44	.71	(.86)	.90

The figures in parentheses are reliabilities of the subtests.

TABLE 2   INTERCORRELATION OF SUBTESTS OF THE IR WITTEN TEST

| | Intercorrelations | | Correlation |
	I	II	with total
Subtest I	(.63)		.87
Subtest II	.64	(.88)	.94

Since the subtests had at most 15 items, one might expect rather small reliability coefficients; the reliabilities were, in fact, of moderate size, and they were thus sufficiently large for the purposes of the study. The tables show that some overlap existed among the different subtests, but each one did account for enough specific variance to be of value and was, therefore, retained. All the subtests also correlated strongly with the test as a whole.

PROCEDURE AND RESULTS

The procedure employed to examine the relationship of SDOS to student achievement consisted of computing class mean scores for all the variables and then comparing these figures. Since each class was a distinct unit and since the material learned by each student could be expected to be influenced by what each teacher taught his class, it was not possible to compare individual students across classes. It was feasible, however, to compute a class mean score on all variables and then compare final student achievement scores for each class and SDOS scores for each teacher with the scores of every other class and teacher, i.e., to examine between class differences.

Table 3 summarizes the class mean scores for the different tests. The range of class means on each different test was great enough to allow for meaningful interpretation of between-class differences.

TABLE 3   TEST STATISTICS FOR CLASSES

	Number of classes	Mean of means	σ	Range of means
MLAT	17	40.43	4.16	33.16 — 48.37
ER	17	28.75	4.04	22.52 — 36.81
IR WRITTEN	17	17.99	2.23	13.19 — 23.81
IR ORAL	17	6.75	1.82	3.50 — 9.31
SDOS*	17	162.5	22.11	127.00 197.00

* These scores are individual teacher scores not class means.

Table 4 summarizes the intercorrelations of the variables. All correlations in Table 4 were based upon class means except for SDOS where the score was for the teacher. In this and succeeding tables, the significance level was the .05 level, but results significant at the .10 level were also identified.

TABLE 4   INTERCORRELATIONS AND MULTIPLE CORRELATIONS OF CLASS MEAN SCORES
(17 CLASSES)

	ER	SDOS	IR WRTN	IR ORAL[b]
MLAT	.57**	−.43*	.42*	.62***
ER		−.68***	.57**	.42*
				(.62***)[c]
SDOS[a]			−.11	−.17
IR WRITTEN				.35
ER, SDOS[d]			.69**	.45
ER, MLAT, SDOS[d]			.71*	.65*

  * = p < .10
  ** = p < .05
  *** = p < .01

[a] SDOS scores are observed scores for each teacher; they are not mean scores.
[b] N per class for this test is smaller than for other tests.
[c] This correlation is between Ir Oral class means and Er class means, but the Er means were computed only for those students who took the oral test.
[d] Multiple correlations.

To reiterate, the purpose of this study was to examine the relationship of SDOS scores to student performance on the criterion tests. Due to the fact that final achievement scores were affected not only by the aptitude level of the class, but also by the prior achievement level of the class as measured by the Er pretest, a multiple regression procedure was required in which it was possible to examine the correlation of one variable with each criterion variable while holding the other variables constant—that is, we wish to examine the partial correlation of each variable (MLAT, Er, SDOS) with each of the criterion variables (Ir Written, and Ir Oral). The correlation of primary interest, as far as the hypothesis of the study was concerned, was the partial correlation of SDOS with Ir Written and of SDOS with Ir Oral. If these correlations turned out to be significant, they would verify the hypothesis that the students of teachers who follow the Sequential Drilling Method more closely achieve better than the students of teachers who do not follow the SDM.

Each of the following tables provides, in addition to the partial correlation, a multiple correlation. This latter coefficient indicates how powerful the three variables (MLAT, Er, SDOS) are, when taken together, in predicting the Ir Written and Ir Oral scores. [Standardized regression weights and their standard errors were also calculated and are available from the author.]

As we mentioned earlier, two of the 17 classes were composed of students who had completed two years of junior-high-school French before entering the high-school first-year French class. In preliminary analyses of the data from all the classes, one of these two classes (Class 17) was shown to be atypical. This preliminary analysis also suggested that a relationship did exist between SDOS and Ir Written, as we hypothesized. When Class 17 was excluded from the data, the hypothesis of a strong relation between Ir Written and SDOS was decisively verified. The partial correlation coefficient was .66***, and the multiple correlation coefficient was .73** (Table 5).

TABLE 5   MULTIPLE REGRESSION ANALYSIS FOR PREDICTING IR-WRITTEN CLASS MEAN FROM ER, MLAT, AND SDOS (N=16[a])

Predictor variable	Type of correlation	Coefficient
Er (SDOS, MLAT constant)	Partial	0.57**
MLAT (Er, SDOS constant)	Partial	0.34
SDOS (Er, MLAT constant)	Partial	0.66***
Er, MLAT, SDOS	Multiple	0.73**

[a] Class 17 deleted.

Table 6 deals with the relation of Ir Oral to the predictors. Neither the partial correlation of Ir Oral with Er nor of Ir Oral with SDOS reached even the .10 level of significance. The partial correlation of Ir Oral with MLAT was significant (0.52**), and this result agreed with the correlation of MLAT with Ir Oral (r=.62**) found in Table 4.

TABLE 6   MULTIPLE REGRESSION ANALYSIS FOR PREDICTING IR-ORAL
CLASS MEAN FROM ER, MLAT, AND SDOS
(N=17)

Predictor variable	Type of correlation	Coefficient
Er (SDOS, MLAT constant)	Partial	0.23
MLAT (Er, SDOS constant)	Partial	0.52**
SDOS (Er, SDOS constant)	Partial	0.24
Er, MLAT, SDOS	Multiple	0.65*

In addition to these main results, one other remarkable finding was obtained; that was the unexpected correlation of −.68*** between SDOS and class means for the Er test (Table 4). The teachers whose students scored higher on the Er pretest ranked consistently lower on SDOS. It is not possible to determine from the data whether teachers who departed from SDM caused high Er scores or whether high ability in the class led teachers to depart from SDM. If we are correct in considering the systematic SDM to be advantageous, the latter is reasonable since the weak class is likely to require a more systematic teaching method.

SUMMARY OF THE RESULTS

The study described in this paper supported the original hypothesis to the extent *that students of teachers who follow the Sequential Drilling Method achieve significantly higher scores in written tests requiring a demonstration of cognition of grammar concepts than comparable students of teachers who follow the SDM less closely when prior ability and aptitude is statistically controlled.* The study was conducted over a short period of time, but the teaching sessions were long enough to adequately teach the grammar concept although not long enough to allow for the development of an ability to use the new forms well in tests of oral ability.

The results for those tests of oral ability, the Ir Oral tests, were not strongly related to SDOS, perhaps because of the small samples used in computing the test scores, but also because the activities required to develop the habitual patterns needed in speaking could not be examined in a study of short duration. The results achieved in the oral test would thus indirectly suggest that activities designed to increase oral fluency should be conducted over a long period of time and that oral ability cannot be achieved in short periods of concentrated drill work. It seems reasonable, therefore, to hypothesize that students of teachers who provide continuous oral drilling according to the Sequential Drilling Method model over a period of weeks, employing in particular higher-level drills, will perform significantly better on oral proficiency tests than students of teachers who provide oral practice which was sequenced in a different manner. Such a hypothesis has not yet, however, been verified.

The Sequential Drilling Observation Scale—developed specifically for this study—has been shown to be a reliable instrument which provides a valid profile of a teacher's drilling procedure. That oral drilling patterns (as expressed by the SDOS scores) are related to the Ir *Written* test scores is initially somewhat astonishing. However, the material introduced and explained early in the drill period was presented visually to the students; it was also referred to by many of the teachers during the oral drilling practice sessions. Many teachers emphasized drilling of the subject pronoun-verb relation, and they did much less drilling with lengthy sentences or in conversational settings—as one might expect in introductory lessons. Students' attention was thus focused on the new forms, and the oral practice stressed structural changes. The drill enhanced recall on the structure and was effective in establishing manipulative abilities, but it did little to further oral proficiency (defined by the Ir Oral test to be the ability to rapidly utter the correct subject pronoun and verb form and to answer simple questions). Thus, even though some of the classes in the study did score very high on the Ir Oral exams, data was not collected over a long enough period to allow us to determine whether teachers of classes which scored high on the Ir Oral test employed a sequentially organized method or whether some entirely different method was employed to aid the students in developing speaking ability.

The most surprising result was the inverse relationship between student performance on the Er written test and the teachers' ability to use oral drills as shown by the SDOS scores. It appears that lower-aptitude classes need to have a very carefully sequenced presentation in order to grasp the new material, a fact which was verified by one teacher of a low-aptitude class who indicated that she had to present material in a very clearly organized pattern to her classes. It was also clear that some teachers of higher-aptitude classes just could not use oral drills effectively in their classes, and some students in these classes complained about a lack of oral work in the classroom.

The problem of poor use of oral drills was not confined to teachers who could not speak the language, since among the teachers who exhibited the poorest drilling performance was a teacher who spoke flawless French outside of the classroom and also one who had very great difficulty speaking the language. The problem lies in the teacher's skill in teaching the foreign language, at least for those teachers who already have an adequate control of the language. For those teachers who have difficulty speaking the language, inability to drill effectively could well be a function of both a lack of knowledge of the language and poor teaching skills.

The reader should bear two considerations in mind when interpreting the results of the study. First, although the results of the study indicate conclusively that student achievement in recall and recognition activities is very significantly higher for classes whose teachers follow the SDM more completely, learning is a complex process, and the obtained results for any of the variables (Er, MLAT, or SDM) are, no doubt, strongly influenced by variables which have not been examined, e.g., by such things as classroom interaction, student motivation, and student attitudes. The effect of outside variables is especially important to consider, since only about 50 percent of the variance among class mean scores is accounted for by the variables studied.

Second, a significant relationship of Ir Oral with SDOS may have been obscured by one or both of two factors affecting the multiple regression analysis of Ir Oral with SDOS. The Ir Oral class mean scores for some classes may be inaccurate because the random samples of students who took the Ir Oral test were quite small for some classes (as small as five students). The second factor of importance, when considering the Ir Oral tests, is the validity of the MLAT scores in the regression, especially since this variable was observed to have the strongest relation to Ir Oral of the three variables examined. Although the MLAT had been validated by the authors of the test for students from ninth to twelfth grade, an undetermined number of students—primarily ninth graders—had difficulty comprehending some of the directions on the Short Form of the MLAT, and may have achieved low scores because they did not know what to do rather than because they were unable to do the work. Thus in further research on the problems examined here or in other studies where MLAT scores are a significant variable, a more careful check on the validity of these scores should be made for the sample used in the study.

IMPLICATIONS

While the study was conducted with students of French, the activities which occur during the teaching of other foreign languages are similar to those employed to teach French; hence, the results stated earlier and the implications for language teaching described in this section are not limited to the teaching of French, but are also applicable to many other modern foreign languages.

Since the results of the study indicate that sequencing oral drills leads to more efficient learning, beginning and also experienced teachers should improve their ability to employ oral drills. Rivers, in her book *The Psychologist and the Foreign Language Teacher*, indicates that pattern drills are "suitable techniques for making foreign-language responses automatic at the manipulative level". She goes on to say that "Composed in language which is of use in real-life situations, with expressions and structures repeated in a variety of contexts, they provide valuable exercise in the active use of the language for the give-and-take of communication" (Rivers, *The Psychologist . . .* , p. 149). She also warns, however, that "In unskilled and unpracticed hands . . . these techniques may become tedious" (p. 149).

A certain amount of dissatisfaction with the quality of oral drills may constitute a major reason for the lower frequency of oral drills and the different sequence of such drills in high-aptitude classes. As we noticed earlier, teachers of high-aptitude classes do not use oral drills in as sequential a manner as the teachers of lower-aptitude classes. No hard data exists to indicate exactly why this should be so, but personal observation and communication with teachers seem to support the belief that high-aptitude classes are able to learn the material whether it is presented sequentially or not. These classes also seem to be more critical of the manner in which oral drilling is conducted, and the students will not tolerate continual repetition, least of all at the "meaningless" manipulative level; continuous rapid variation in the oral drills is essential, and this activity requires special skills on the part of the teacher. Conversely, lower-aptitude classes need a much more sequential presentation of the material and more repetition of the same material. However, since the results of the study indicate that students at any aptitude level profit from a sequentially organized presentation, the following conclusions can be drawn. First, although the students of high-aptitude classes do learn the material, the teachers of these classes do a poorer job of oral drilling or, stated another way, they are not highly enough skilled in oral drilling techniques to meet the demands placed on them by their students. Second, since sequential oral drilling is a more efficient method of learning for high- as well as low-aptitude classes, the teachers of high-aptitude classes definitely need to improve their drilling skills. Third, teachers of low-aptitude classes need to further refine their skills so that they could handle high-aptitude classes as well as improve their effectiveness in the low-aptitude classes.

How does a teacher improve his use of oral drills? For beginning teachers, the best way to improve is through effective training in teacher-education programs. For other teachers, inservice and self-improvement programs can be employed. Certain materials are available which provide practical suggestions for the teacher. (See Note at end of this paper.)

In addition to these more general materials, a teacher can use the SDOS to obtain a drilling profile of his own drilling activities, and I have listed a few guidelines for interpreting the profile in the article "The Sequential Drilling Observation Scale". For example, the profile should show a general trend toward use of drills at a higher degree as the drilling period progresses so that the teacher is not always using repetition drills and other manipulative drills, but progresses to longer question-and-answer sequences (Morrey, "The Sequential . . .", p. 12).

Not only should the single drilling session exhibit such a trend from manipulative to communicative activities, but also this trend should be evident in the different drills of the elementary, intermediate and advanced language classes. As Prator says, the progression from manipulative to communicative activities "should characterize the movement from elementary to advanced instruction, with manipulation predominating in the former and communication in the latter." Prator goes on to say that most students, as they go from beginning to advanced courses, do not go through a gradual transition period in which the emphasis shifts from manipulative drills of the elementary period (Prator advocates some simple communicative activities even here) to communicative activities of the advanced period. (Prator, "Guidelines for Planning Classes and Teaching Materials", p. 27.)

In the preceding discussion, the need for better sequencing and use of drills was stated and a few procedures were given for improving the effectiveness of oral drill work. The suggestions made above apply primarily to drill work with elementary classes in which the manipulative activities are stressed. As far as communicative activities are concerned, the study provides only indirect evidence that communicative ability is developed through long-term activities. However, Rivers also considers the development of speaking ability to be a lengthy process (Rivers, *Teaching* . . . , p. 160).

If we consider communication in a foreign language to be a skill activity much like typing or playing an instrument, it is understandable that students have to practice speaking over a period of time before they are able to actually communicate. Rivers says that "Students in a foreign-language class will not learn to speak fluently merely by hearing speech . . . The teacher will need to give the student many opportunities to practice the speaking skill" (Rivers, *Teaching* . . . , p. 160). Rivers adds that "The teaching of the speaking skill . . . involves two levels of activity. The forging of the instrument requires much practice in the arbitrary associations of the new language. . . . At this level the student is asked merely to manipulate the elements of the foreign-language code, so that he can express a number of possible meanings arbitrarily imposed upon him by the exercise or the teacher. When he has acquired facility in these mechanical associations, he needs practice in setting in motion a number of interacting systems of a hierarchical nature. . . ." (Rivers, *Teaching* . . . , p. 162). In other words, students must not only participate actively in communicative activities, but they must have a strong foundation upon which to progress, i.e., extensive practice at the manipulative level.

As the student progresses from manipulative drills to communicative activities, what forms do these activities take? I describe a few communicative activities in the article "Successive Degrees of Difficulty in Oral Drills: Their Use in the Classroom". In addition to these activities, small conversation groups can be formed which are composed of students with approximately the same level of conversational ability. One procedure is to provide the students in a group with a short text appropriate to their ability three or four days before the group meets. The students read the material a few times to become familiar with the contents prior to the group meeting. Then in the conversational group the students answer questions based on the text or perhaps retell in their own words what happened in the story.

Up until this point, we have been primarily discussing the use of oral drills at various points in the foreign-language sequence. We have seen how the SDM provides an efficient method of organizing the drills for the class period or even for several days or weeks. The SDM can also be regarded as an organizing framework for Prator's "gradual transition" from manipulative to communicative activities as the students move from beginning to intermediate and advanced levels of instruction. Used in this way, the SDM would indicate that the majority of oral drills in the very early stages of instruction are manipulative with a very few at the communicative level. As the student acquires a broader background in the language, there is less need for extensive manipulative drills and the emphasis gradually shifts to communication. At the intermediate and even more so at the advanced levels, manipulative drills are used only to introduce new concepts, vocabulary or similar new material. Since progressively less new material is introduced at the more advanced levels of instruction, the necessity for manipulative drills is reduced. Conversely, as the students acquire more material, there is an ever–increasing need to practice this material, and communicative activities become more important.

The SDM has value beyond its use as an organizing concept of oral drills in the classroom; it provides a framework for organizing oral and written drills in materials used in individualized instruction (and also as a guideline for evaluating the structure of such materials). As individualization of instruction becomes more and more widespread, more teachers will prepare their own materials, or at least some of them. If these teachers, and others who prepare such materials, arrange drills and exercises in a manner consistent with the SDM, a more effective set of materials can be developed.

The results of the study reported in this article strongly indicate that the use of oral drills according to the SDM model does affect student achievement, at least for activities requiring recall of the material learned. Whether the SDM is also effective in promoting speaking abilities over the long term is at this point still undetermined. The teacher needs to become aware of the great variety of oral drills available and learn how to use them effectively in order to improve the achievement of his students. The SDM can also be regarded as an organizational framework for structuring drills and exercises in new materials, which the teacher may write, as well as during oral drilling periods in the classroom. The SDM is widely applicable and provides teachers with clear guidelines for use of oral drills in their foreign-language program.

NOTE

A list of some of the most specific practical sources dealing with the structure and sequence of material in oral drills is presented below:

Rivers, Wilga M. *The Psychologist and the Foreign-Language Teacher.* Chicago: The University of Chicago Press, 1964, Chapter 13.

————. *Teaching Foreign-Language Skills.* Chicago: The University of Chicago Press, 1969, Chapters 7-8.

Politzer, Robert L. *Teaching French: An Introduction to Applied Linguistics.* New York: Blaisdell Publishing Co., 1960.

————. *Foreign Language Learning: A Linguistic Introduction.* Englewood Cliffs, N.J.: Prentice-Hall, Inc., 1965.

————. *Practice-Centered Teacher Training: French.* Stanford Center for Research and Development in Teaching, Technical Report No. 1, 1966.

————. *Practice-Centered Teacher Training: Spanish.* Stanford Center for Research and Development in Teaching, Technical Report No. 2, 1967.

Quilter, Daniel N. *Do's and Don't's of Audio-Lingual Teaching.* Blaisdell, 1966.

REFERENCES

Brooks, Nelson. *Language and Language Learning.* 2nd ed., New York: Harcourt, Brace and World, Inc., 1964, Chapter 11.

Huebener, Theodore. *How to Teach Foreign Languages Effectively.* Rev. ed., New York: New York University Press, 1965, 19-23.

Lado, Robert. *Language Teaching: A Scientific Approach.* New York: McGraw-Hill Book Co., 1964, 90-113.

Morrey, Robert A. "Successive Degrees of Difficulty in Oral Drills: Their Use in the Classroom." *American Foreign Language Teacher,* 1:2, 1970, 6-11.

————. "The Sequential Drilling Observation Scale." Unpublished article.

Oliva, Peter F. *The Teaching of Foreign Languages.* Englewood Cliffs, N.J.: Prentice-Hall, Inc., 1969, Chapter 6.

Paulston, Christina Bratt. "Structural Pattern Drills: A Classification." *Foreign Language Annals,* 4:2 (1970), 187-193.

Politzer, Robert L. *Teaching French: An Introduction to Applied Linguistics.* New York: Blaisdell Publishing Co., 1964, 23-27.

————. *Foreign Language Learning: A Linguistic Introduction.* Englewood Cliffs, N.J.: Prentice-Hall, Inc., 1965, Chapter 14.

————. "The Effective Use of the Structure Drill." *The French Review,* 38:5, 1965, 677-680.

————. *Performance Criteria for the Foreign Language Teacher.* Technical Report No. 1A, Stanford Center for Research and Development in Teaching.

————. "Toward Psycholinguistic Models of Language Instruction." *TESOL Quarterly*, 2:3, 1968, 154.

Prator, Clifford H. "Development of a Manipulation-Communication Scale." In: *The 1964 Conference Papers of the Association of Teachers of English as a Second Language of the National Association for Foreign Student Affairs*. Ed. Robert P. Fox. New York: The National Association for Foreign Student Affairs, 57-62.

————. "Guidelines for Planning Classes and Teaching Materials." In: *Workpapers in ESL: Matter, Methods, Materials*. Department of English, UCLA, April, 1967.

Rivers, Wilga M. *Teaching Foreign-Language Skills*. Chicago: The University of Chicago Press, 1968.

————. *The Psychologist and the Foreign-Language Teacher*. Chicago: The University of Chicago Press, 1964.

MICHAEL D. OATES*

A Syntactic Classification of French Verbs as a Basis for Monostructural Presentation at the Beginning Level

No method can take the place of the skilled teacher who succeeds in dispelling inhibition and in encouraging his students to communicate in the foreign language. But in addition to a capable, motivating teacher, students of French should be provided with pedagogically sound materials which are based on an accurate linguistic description. It is felt by the author of this article that the most pedagogically attractive approach is one which presents utterance-length material and which permits a student to focus his attention on one unit at a time: a monostructural presentation of French sentences.

A monostructural presentation of grammar need not be oversimplified and unnatural (Grittner, 1969, p. 126). We should not force students to spend weeks discussing yellow pencils, new books, brown tables, etc. Hopefully, the choice of vocabulary will allow students to talk about themselves and others rather than about the physical makeup of their classroom.

Assuredly, one of the most often repeated criticisms of the audio-lingual method is that, in spite of the great amount of time spent drilling the basic dialogues, many students do not grasp the structure

---

* University of Northern Iowa.

of the material they are drilling. It is therefore common to find secondary-school students of French who are quite able to give a set answer when the proper cue is present. The same, however, often cannot cope with a question which is not in the exact pre-learned order. Pupil and teacher dissatisfaction with the results achieved have caused some to lose heart and to fall back on lengthy grammatical explanations and verb charts. Perhaps what should be questioned is the multi-structured approach used in the basic dialogue materials.

Present audiolingual texts often hamper learning by presenting a multiplicity of different structures in beginning lessons. This is especially true of the "slice of life" type of dialogue found in the most popular texts. Elliptical sentences as well as compound and complex sentences are used together. Negative and interrogative sentences are found together with declarative sentences from the beginning. Transitive, intransitive and equational clauses are present in lesson one.

Primacy has been given to the veracity of the material. Chief concern is therefore that the material resemble a normal conversation between two native speakers of the learner's age. And yet, the language learner is not a native speaker of the foreign language. While the materials may please teachers of French because of their Gallic flavor, the end results are too often lacking. The structural complexity of the material used does not facilitate extrapolation. Students eventually discover that, in spite of lengthy drills, they are often unable to use the material presented to express their ideas, feelings, emotions.

Why abandon the pedagogical principle "teach one thing at a time and teach it well"? There is a need to establish a solid basis which will permit students to grasp each pattern. Certainly, the students should be exposed to real native-speaker conversations "prises sur le vif". These conversations will undoubtedly include elliptical sentences as well as a multiplicity of differing structural patterns. However, as William Moulton states (1970, p. 67), at the start "it is better to concentrate on the really basic productive sentence types."

In his *Trends in Language Teaching*, Albert Valdman (1966, p. xx) signals the need for pedagogically oriented grammars. He states (1966, p. xxi) "A pedagogical grammar will use whatever grammatical theory proves most useful for a specific aspect of the structure of the language". He adds that, to his knowledge, there is no syntactic classification of French verbs to account for the types of sentences that are expected of beginning and intermediate learners.

French verbs are typically classified on morphological grounds. Those verbs with the present tense endings "e", "es", "e", "ons", etc.

and the infinitive ending "er" are classed together as "ER" verbs. Separate lessons are often headed "ER verbs", "IR verbs", "RE verbs", and "Irregular verbs". Often students have been forced to wait to use such frequent verbs as *aller, vouloir, pouvoir,* and *croire* because these verbs do not fit the neat "ER", "IR" or "RE" classes.

Why begin at the word level when classifying verbs? Since it is deemed desirable to have students learn complete utterances, should not the classification of a verb be based on the way it is used in utterances rather than on the endings which it takes? Why not group verbs according to the types of sentences in which they are used? A different classification should result from the one based on morphology. The verbs *partir, dîner, dormir,* and *ronfler,* for example, would most likely be classed together since they are used in the same structural pattern: S + P, subject plus predicate. None of these verbs admit the use of a direct or an indirect object.

By grouping verbs according to their structural potential, rather than on the basis of morphological considerations, account would be taken of the deep structural functioning of the verbs. They would be seen to occur in some constructions but not in others. Such a study would entail an analysis of French clause types. The clauses can be used as a sieve through which verbs would be sorted into classes based on the same structural potential. The results should suggest a blueprint for a monostructural approach in the presentation of French to beginning students. One might wish to present new material one structure at a time, choosing the most frequent verbs which can fit the pattern being presented.

This article will be limited to the fifty most frequent verbs found in the corpus of *Le Français Fondamental* (Gougenheim 1964). The fifty most frequent verbs, as listed by Rivenc (1968, p. 29) in order of decreasing occurrence, are:

être	croire	rester	rendre
avoir	mettre	manger	revenir
faire	passer	appeler	lire
dire	devoir	sortir	monter
aller	trouver	travailler	payer
voir	donner	acheter	parler
savoir	comprendre	laisser	chercher
pouvoir	connaître	écouter	jouer
falloir	partir	entendre	paraître
vouloir	demander	rentrer	attendre
venir	tenir	commencer	perdre
prendre	aimer	marcher	
arriver	penser	regarder	

Among the first 15 verbs there is only one, *arriver*, which belongs to a regular conjugation. The traditional presentation of regular verbs before irregular verbs taught the less frequent verbs first. The results of the above-mentioned frequency study do not support such an approach to the teaching of verbs. It could be argued that regular verbs should be taught first since the overwhelming majority of French verbs are regular. Indeed, new verbs do·seem to be formed by adding orthographic *er* to a noun stem: *solutionner, émotionner* (Martinet, 1969, p. 42) by analogy with the vast number of verbs in *er*. The most commonly occurring verbs are, however, irregular and the proof of their frequency is that they have been able to withstand the pressure from analogy. In the above list, there are no regular *ir* verbs and only four regular *re* verbs: *entendre, rendre, attendre,* and *perdre*. A student who has mastered only the regular conjugations of French is incapable of producing the most commonly used sentences.

The argument should perhaps not be focused on the morphology of the verbs. If our task were solely to learn the endings of verbs, we should indeed begin with that which is regular. But if speaking the language is a chief goal, primary concern must be given to the way a verb performs in context. In what type of constructions can the verb be used? This article will attempt to describe the syntactic relationships of the fifty most frequent verbs.

THE THEORY

The tagmemic theory, which makes explicit form, function, and distribution in a construction, is pedagogically most useful in setting up the basic types of constructions in French. In the tagmemic model (Pike 1967, Longacre 1964, Cook 1969), the unit or tagmeme is a correlation of function and form which is distributed in the constructions of a language. The constructions are made up of a string of tagmemes, and each construction serves, in turn, as a filler class found typically on a higher level. The levels are those of sentence, clause, phrase, word, and morpheme.

By limiting syntactic description to those sentences which are simple, complete, affirmative, active and statements, one can concentrate on the basic elements in the constructions.

Initial breakdown begins at the sentence level:

SENT = +Base −Into

That is, a sentence is divided into a base and an intonation.

The tagmeme whose function is that of base may have as a filler a transitive, intransitive, or equational clause:

SENT = +Base:tCl/iCl/eqCl −Into:ICF

That is, a sentence is composed of a base slot, filled by a transitive, intransitive, or equational clause and an intonation slot, filled by a final intonation contour.

When analyzing the clause level, the function of a verb must first be determined. Is the verb functioning as an auxiliary? For example:

J'ai dansé

Or is the verb functioning as the predicate? For example:

J'ai cinq francs.

The list of most frequently occurring verbs includes many which may function as auxiliaries either with the past participle: *avoir, être* or with an infinitive: *aller, savoir, pouvoir,* etc. A simplification in description will result by distinguishing between the use of a verb with a participle or an infinitive:

je sais danser

and its use with other words, phrases or clauses:

je sais cela
je sais ma leçon
je sais qui vous êtes.

Jean Dubois (1967, p. 11) gives the example *Paul va venir demain.* He refers to the group *va venir* as the *syntagme verbal,* "the verb phrase". In his analysis, *va* is designated as the verb and *venir* is termed *une forme nominale,* "a noun-like form". He does not go as far as to call this infinitive an object. To do so would be contrary to its usage in other constructions since *aller,* with the exception of the expression *s'en aller,* is never found with a direct object. Dubois (1967, p. 19) does, however, refer to *à travailler* in *Il continue à travailler* as the object of the verb *continue.* He does so since *à travailler* could be replaced by the noun phrase *son travail* which functions as the direct object of *continue.*

It would seem, however, desirable to treat both *va venir* and *continue à travailler* in the same way. Rather than say that *à travailler* is an object while *venir* is not, both constructions could be treated in the same fashion by considering them as verb phrases, with *va* and *continue* acting as auxiliaries.

Thus in the case of *Paul va venir*:

iCL = +S:n +P:iV

That is, this intransitive clause construction is composed of an obligatory subject slot, filled by a noun, and an obligatory predicate slot, filled by an intransitive verb phrase.

In the case of the verb phrase *va venir*:

iV = +Aux: iv +H: iinf

That is, this intransitive verb phrase construction is composed of an obligatory auxiliary slot, filled by an intransitive verb, and an obligatory head slot, filled by an intransitive infinitive.

The above description parallels the treatment of *avoir* and *être* with the past participle. In the case of *Paul est arrivé:*

iCl = +S:n +P:iV

iV = +Aux: eqv +H: ipp

That is, this intransitive verb phrase is composed of an obligatory auxiliary slot, filled by an equation verb, and an obligatory head slot, filled by an intransitive past participle.

Both the infinitive *venir* and the past participle *arrivé* are marked above to show whether or not they are transitive. It is the form which functions as the head of the verb phrase which governs the occurrence of objects. In the case of the following two examples, there is an object:

> *Paul va voir son ami*
>
> *Paul a commencé ses devoirs*

In both cases, the clause structure is the same:

tCl = +S:n +P:tV ±DO:N

That is, this transitive clause construction is composed of an obligatory subject slot, filled by a noun, an obligatory predicate slot, filled by a transitive verb phrase, and an optional direct object slot, filled by a noun phrase. In both cases, the direct object is governed by the second element of the predicate. The auxiliaries govern no objects of their own. This is, then, the criterion used in this study to distinguish an auxiliary from a verb which functions as predicate all by itself: a verb used as an auxiliary cannot take an object.

In the list of the fifty most frequent verbs, the following can be used as auxiliaries:

être	pouvoir	devoir	commencer
avoir	vouloir	tenir	chercher
aller	venir	aimer	
savoir	croire	penser	

For example: *Je suis tombé*

> *Je les ai vus*
>
> *Il sait danser*
>
> *Il peut le faire*

Objects, when present, are governed solely by the head of the verb phrase. When the object slot is filled by a pronoun, its distribution depends on whether the head of the verb phrase is a past participle or an infinitive. Pronoun objects precede the auxiliary when the head is a past participle:

> *je l'ai trouvé.*

They precede the head when it is an infinitive:

je vais le regarder
je tiens à le faire

Etre and *avoir* may also be used as auxiliaries with an infinitive:

j'ai à le faire
j'ai été le voir

In addition to the above-mentioned verbs which can be used as auxiliaries, there are other verbs in the list of fifty which can be followed by an infinitive. For example:

je lui dis de chanter
il nous fait étudier la leçon
il nous faut venir

The verbs *dis, fait,* and *faut* should not be classed as auxiliaries. They are all capable of having an object. Furthermore this object, when a pronoun, is placed before the verb rather than before the infinitive. The infinitive, together with its objects, can be considered as the direct object of the verb:

tCl = +S: pn ±IO: pn +P: tv +DO: Inf

That is, these transitive clause constructions consist of an obligatory subject slot, filled by a pronoun, an optional indirect object slot, filled by a pronoun, an obligatory predicate slot, filled by a transitive verb, and an obligatory direct object slot, filled by an infinitive phrase.

In the list of the fifty most frequent verbs, the following can be used with an infinitive as object:

faire	demander	regarder
dire	laisser	paraître
voir	écouter	
falloir	entendre	

It might be argued that *donner* should also be added to this list. It can be followed by an infinitive phrase. For example:

Je leur donne à boire.

Structurally, it is the same as the sentence

Je lui dis de chanter:

tCl = +S:pn ±IO:pn +P:tv +DO: Inf

However, the infinitive phrase *à boire* in the above sentence is an ellipsis of the noun phrase *quelque chose à boire.* This is not the case for the infinitive phrase *de chanter. Donner* is therefore not included in the list of verbs given above.

The other verbs in the list of fifty are either never followed by the infinitive, for example: *trouver* and *perdre,* or they allow its use only when the word *pour* could be inserted before the infinitive. For example: *rentrer, Je rentre dîner.*

As an initial step in the analysis of the fifty most frequently used verbs in French, the use of a verb with a participle or an infinitive has been distinguished from its use with other words, phrases, or clauses. Three syntactic classes have been established: the use of a verb as an auxiliary in a verb phrase when the head is a past participle, the use of a verb as an auxiliary in a verb phrase when the head is an infinitive, and the use of a verb as a predicate followed by an infinitive functioning as direct object. In addition, some verbs are not used with an infinitive.

TABLE 1: 50 VERBS CLASSED ACCORDING TO THEIR USE WITH AN INFINITIVE OR A PARTICIPLE

As auxiliary with past participle	As auxiliary with infinitive	With infinitive as DO		Normally without an infinitive
être	être	croire	faire	prendre	travailler
avoir	avoir	devoir	dire	arriver	acheter
	aller	tenir	voir	mettre	rentrer
	savoir	aimer	falloir	passer	marcher
	pouvoir	penser	demander	trouver	rendre
	vouloir	commencer	laisser	donner	revenir
	venir	chercher	écouter	comprendre	lire
			entendre	connaître	monter
			regarder	partir	payer
			paraître	rester	parler
				manger	jouer
				appeler	attendre
				sortir	perdre

The above classes are based on the use of verbs with infinitives and past participles. Verbs must also be classed according to the other forms with which they may occur. As part of this classification, the basic clause types of French will have to be established. Once this is accomplished, the fifty verbs can be examined to determine in which clauses they may occur.

In tagmemic analysis, clauses are distinguished on the basis of their essential, or nuclear, parts. Non-nuclear, or peripheral, tagmemes are those which are not diagnostic of the constructions in which they occur. Adverbials and other adjuncts are normally peripheral in French. They add information in answer to such questions as *quand?*,

où?, comment?, combien?, combien de fois?, etc. They are not ordi-
narily part of the nucleus. The nuclear tagmemes at the clause level
in French are subject, predicate, direct object, indirect object, objective complement, and predicate attribute (Oates 1970). They
form the essential parts of French clause constructions when syntactic description is limited to those sentences which are simple,
complete, affirmative, active statements.

Taking into consideration only the nuclear parts of French clauses,
at least eight basic clause types may be distinguished. There are five
transitive clauses types, two intransitive clause types and one equational clause type.

To somewhat simplify the following description of basic clause
types in French, the word *phrase* is used to include both phrases and
single words which may be replaced by a phrase.

TRANSITIVE CLAUSES

Distinctions in the transitive depend not only on the type of
transitive verb present but also on the nuclear element which follows the predicate. This nuclear element may be an obligatory or
optional direct object. There may also be an indirect object or an
objective complement present.

TYPE ONE

$$tCl_1 = +S:N +P:tV_1 +DO:N$$

That is, a transitive type-one clause construction is one in which
there is an obligatory subject slot, filled by a noun phrase, an obligatory predicate slot, filled by a type-one transitive verb phrase,
and an obligatory direct object slot, filled by a noun phrase. For
example:

> *Inès a sorti ses griffes*
> *J'ai mal*
> *Il a bien descendu les premières marches*
> *Nous monterons la même selle*

The above verbs: *sortir, avoir, descendre*, and *monter* are type-one
transitive verbs since they require a direct object. As tV_1 class members, *sortir, descendre*, and *monter* are conjugated in past compound
tenses with the auxiliary *avoir*. They should not be confused with
those constructions in which *sortir, descendre*, and *monter* are conjugated with *être* and do not allow an object.

TYPE TWO

$$tCl_2 = +S:N +P:tV_2 \pm DO:N$$

That is, a transitive type-two clause construction is one in which there is an obligatory subject slot, filled by a noun phrase, an obligatory predicate slot, filled by a type-two transitive verb phrase, and an optional direct object slot, filled by a noun phrase. For example:

Je file
Nous filerons la scène
J'ai tué
J'en ai tué trois

The above verbs, *filer* and *tuer*, are type-two transitive verbs since they are used with or without a direct object.

TYPE THREE

$$tCl_3 = +S{:}N +P{:}tV_3 +DO{:}N \pm OC{:}N/Aj$$

That is, a transitive type-three clause construction is one in which there is an obligatory subject slot, filled by a noun phrase, an obligatory predicate slot, filled by a type-three transitive verb phrase, an obligatory direct object, filled by a noun phrase, and an optional objective complement slot, filled by either a noun phrase or an adjective phrase. For example:

Je trouve la scène un peu grosse
J'ai rendu les choses plus difficiles

The connection between the objective complement and the direct object may be seen by the gender and number concord evidenced between *la scène* and *un peu grosse* and between *les choses* and *plus difficiles*. Relatively few transitive verbs have the possibility of taking an objective complement.

TYPE FOUR

$$tCl_4 = +S{:}N +P{:}tV_4 +DO{:}N \pm IO{:} RA$$

That is, a transitive type-four clause construction is one in which there is an obligatory subject slot, filled by a noun phrase, an obligatory predicate slot, filled by a type-four transitive verb phrase, an obligatory direct object slot, filled by a noun phrase, and an optional indirect object slot, filled by a relater-axis phrase (preposition plus noun phrase). For example:

L'Inquisition laisse le soin aux évêques
Je fais peur à tout le monde
Pavel remettra un message au portier

The above verbs, *laisser*, *faire*, and *remettre*, are type-four transitive verbs since they require an obligatory direct object and since they may also be followed by an indirect object. They differ from type-five transitive verbs in that the direct object may be omitted with the type-five transitive verbs.

TYPE FIVE

$$tCl_5 = +S:N +P:tV_5 \pm DO:N \pm IO:RA$$

That is, a transitive type-five clause construction is one in which there is an obligatory subject slot, filled by a noun phrase, an obligatory predicate slot, filled by a type-five transitive verb phrase, an optional direct object slot, filled by a noun phrase, and an optional indirect object slot, filled by a relater-axis phrase. For example:

Ils lui ont chanté une chanson
Il a écrit une lettre à sa mère
Elle parle français à ses étudiants

INTRANSITIVE CLAUSES

Distinctions in the intransitive clauses depend on both the type of intransitive verb present and on whether or not there is an indirect object present.

TYPE ONE

$$iCl_1 = +S:N +P:iV_1$$

That is, an intransitive type-one clause construction is one in which there is an obligatory subject slot, filled by a noun phrase, and an obligatory predicate slot, filled by a type-one intransitive verb phrase. For example:

Il est parti
J'ai dormi
Elle est morte tout à l'heure
Vous êtes entrée

TYPE TWO

$$iCl_2 = +S:N +P:iV_2 \pm IO:RA$$

That is, an intransitive type-two clause construction is one in which there is an obligatory subject slot, filled by a noun phrase, an obligatory predicate slot, filled by a type-two intransitive verb phrase, and an optional indirect object slot, filled by a relater-axis phrase. For example:

J'obéis à la police
Ce chapeau lui va bien

Other intransitive clauses are possible but seem to be restricted to one verb only. The verb *parler*, for example, may be used with two indirect objects:

Tu me parles de Dieu

The verb *ressembler* differs from the iV_2 class in that it requires an indirect object. For example:

Il ressemble à son père

EQUATIONAL CLAUSES

There is one basic type of equational clause. The predicate attribute slot may be filled by three different phrase types.

eqCl = +S:N +P:eqV +PA:N/Aj/Av

That is, an equational clause construction is one in which there is an obligatory subject slot, filled by a noun phrase, an obligatory predicate slot, filled by an equational verb phrase, and an obligatory predicate attribute slot, filled by either a noun phrase, or an adjective phrase, or an adverb phrase. For example:

> *J'ai été lâche*
> *Elle redevient une petite fille*
> *Vous êtes là*

Occasionally equational verbs may be found with optional indirect objects. For example:

> *Cela m'est difficile*
> *Il me semble un peu distrait*

The above description has postulated eight basic clause types in French. The fifty most frequent verbs can now be examined to determine in which of these clauses they may occur.

Many of the verbs are found to occur in more than one of the eight clause types. The case of *sortir*, tV_1 and iV_1, has already been noted. Likewise, it seems best to analyze the verb *payer* as belonging to more than one class. It can be tV_4: *je paie l'addition au garçon.* Furthermore the indirect object is not found with the verb unless there is a direct object present. If there is only one object, it is direct: *Je paie le garçon.* But this verb can also be found without an object: *C'est moi qui paie.* It must therefore also be classed as tV_2.

Likewise *rendre* is classed as tV_2: *le bébé a rendu (tout son déjeuner),* as tV_3: *cela me rend malade,* and as tV_4: *il nous a rendu le livre.*

The following classification does not include a description of the verbs when they are followed by an infinitive. Classes of verbs based on their role with an infinitive or a participle have been discussed above.

THE USE OF THE FIFTY VERBS

IN THE BASIC CLAUSES

1: $P:tV_1$ +DO

avoir	connaître	rentrer
croire	tenir	monter
trouver	sortir	

For example: *Nous avons cinq francs*
Elle connaît bien ma mère
Il tient un livre sous le bras
Il a rentré sa voiture au garage

2: P:tV$_2$ ±DO

voir	aimer	entendre
savoir	penser	commencer
pouvoir	manger	regarder
vouloir	travailler	attendre
comprendre	écouter	perdre

For example: *Je voudrais un livre*
Je veux bien
Il attend sa femme
Il attend
Ils ont perdu le match
Ils ont perdu

3: P:tV$_3$ +DO ±OC

croire	appeler
trouver	rendre

For example: *Georges se croit un bon professeur*
Il croit cette histoire
Ils m'ont appelée vilaine
Elle a appelé son fils

4: P:tV$_4$ +DO ±IO

faire	passer	laisser
dire	devoir	rendre
falloir	donner	chercher
prendre	demander	jouer
mettre	acheter	

For example: *Il lui faut une bonne*
Il faut encore cinq francs
Nous avons acheté ce livre au libraire
Ils ont acheté une voiture
Il m'a mis mon manteau
Il a mis son pardessus

5: P:tV$_5$ ±DO ±IO

parler	lire

For example: *Il leur a lu l'histoire*
                 Il a lu l'histoire
                 Il leur a lu
                 Il a lu

6: P:iV$_1$

aller	partir	marcher
venir	tenir	revenir
arriver	sortir	monter
donner	rentrer	paraître

For example: *Il va en ville*
                 Nous marchons depuis longtemps
                 Elle est partie hier
                 La fenêtre donne sur la rue
                 L'écrou tient encore
                 Ce livre a paru l'année dernière

7: P:iV$_2$ ±IO

aller	penser	jouer
croire	rester	

For example: *Nous croyons en nos professeurs*
                 Il croit sans raison
                 La robe lui va bien
                 Il joue du piano
                 Il pense à son vieux père

8: P:eqV +PA

être	faire	paraître

For example: *Il est professeur*
                 Il fera un bon médecin
                 Dans cette robe elle fait très jeune
                 Son père paraît très sévère

The fifty most frequent verbs were initially subdivided on the basis of their use with an infinitive or a participle. Three syntactic classes were established on that basis. The verbs were next subdivided on the basis of their occurrence in the basic clause structures of French. Eight syntactic classes were established.

There was some overlapping when several verbs were found to occur in two or three different clause constructions. It was felt that in some cases a verb could not fit in one syntactic slot alone. Such was the case with *donner*. The role and the meaning of this verb in sentences of the type *la fenêtre donnait sur le court de tennis* are essentially different from its role and meaning in sentences of the type *il a donné un livre à son frère.* The first example was classed as an iV_1; the second as a tV_4. To try and lump both sentences together in a tV_5 construction would equate two uses which are essentially different. *Donner* in the first sentence can not have an object. *Donner* in the second sentence must always have a direct object.

Decisions of the type made for *donner* were also made for the verbs *aller, croire, trouver, tenir, penser, sortir, rentrer, rendre, monter,* and *paraître.* Another analysis of the same list of verbs might determine that there are others which should be placed in more than one class. Should it prove pedagogically useful to do so, such an analysis should be encouraged. The above analysis has, however, tried to limit itself to the most common expressions in which the fifty verbs can be found.

Some uses were omitted which might have to be introduced during a beginning course. This was certainly the case for the expression *je m'en vais.* To include it in the study would have required analyzing *aller* as a transitive verb. While theoretically this would be the best decision, it would not be wise pedagogically. *Aller* is transitive only when found in the above construction. Furthermore, its direct object must be a pronoun: *tu t'en vas, il s'en va,* etc. It was therefore decided not to include it in the data.

At least eleven different constructions can then be distinguished for the fifty most frequent verbs in French.

PEDAGOGICAL IMPLICATIONS

The syntactic role of the verb should determine the way in which material is grouped and presented at the beginning level. The morphological class of the verb is of secondary but nevertheless important consideration. The order of presentation within a class of syntactically similar verbs can be based on morphological grounds. Therefore *pouvoir* and *vouloir,* which are classed together on the basis of their use as auxiliaries, should be taught at the same time. Both of these verbs show the /ø,u,oe/ vowel alternation in the present: *peux, pouvons peuvent.* Likewise, both of the verbs form the past participle in /y/.

The traditional grouping of verbs conjugated with *être* is valuable on both morphological and syntactical grounds. Morphologically, they are grouped since they are used with the auxiliary *être* in compound tenses and the past participle agrees with the subject. Syntactically, they are grouped since they can function as iV_1.

TABLE 2:   THE 11 BASIC CONSTRUCTIONS

1. +S:N +P:(Aux + Inf)
   Il va partir.

2. +S:N +P:(Aux + pp)
   Il est parti.

3. +S:N +P:V +DO:Inf
   Il a dit (à son frère) de le faire.

4. +S:N +P:tV_1 +DO:N
   Il a monté l'escalier.

5. +S:N +P:tV_2 ±DO:N
   Ils ont mangé un bifteck.

6. +S:N +P:tV_3 +DO:N ±OC:N/Aj
   Je l'ai trouvé intéressant.

7. +S:N +P:tV_4 +DO:N ±IO:RA
   Il a donné deux dollars à son frère.

8. +S:N +P:tV_5 ±DO:N ±IO:RA
   Elle lui parle espagnol.

9. +S:N +P:iV_1
   Son frère est revenu.

10. +S:N +P:iV_2 ±IO:RA
    Il pense à son ami.

11. +S:N +P:eqV +PA:N/Aj/Av
    Il paraît assez intelligent.

Due to their frequent use and similar syntactic behavior, the
"être" verbs should be presented early in the beginning course.
Several of them may also be found as tV_1 verbs in +S:N +P:tV_1
+DO:N constructions: *sortir, rentrer, monter.* Their use as tV_1 verbs
should be contrasted with their use as iV_1 verbs once the past composed tense has been introduced:

tV_1 *Elle a sorti le livre*
iV_1 *Elle est sortie*

Donner, tenir, marcher, and *paraître* were the only iV_1 verbs which
did not belong to the morphologically classed *"être"* verbs. *Paraître*
may be conjugated with *être: la nouvelle édition est parue.* It is
however normally found with *avoir,* and most importantly, its use as
an iV_1 verb seems much less frequent than its use as an eqV: *cela
paraît difficile. Paraître* should perhaps therefore be taught only as
an eqV on the beginning level. *Donner* and *tenir* may likewise be
found in other constructions. Their use with direct objects, *il a
donné de l'argent, il tenait son livre,* seems not only more frequent

but also more pedagogically useful than their use in the iV$_1$ construction. *Marcher,* however, occurs only as an iV$_1$ verb. It must be taught early and contrasted with the iV$_1$ *"être"* verbs.

With the exception of *avoir* and *être,* those verbs which may be used as auxiliaries should perhaps initially be presented in this role. If *pouvoir, vouloir, devoir,* etc. are among the most frequently used verbs in French, it is due in large part to their use as auxiliaries. The sentences *il doit partir* and *il veut danser* would then be presented before the sentences *il doit cinq francs* and *il veut un livre.* While the verbs *vouloir, pouvoir, devoir,* etc. have a similar function when used as auxiliaries, they do not have the same function when used with direct and indirect objects.

Avoir and *être* are used much less with the infinitive than with the past participle. Since one would not wish to present the past compound tenses prior to the present tense, *avoir* and *être* should first be presented in their role as main verb, *j'ai des amis, il est professeur,* prior to their role as auxiliaries.

Special stress should be placed on those verbs which are syntactic *faux amis* of their English equivalents. In the list of fifty verbs, at least the following should be marked as syntactically different from their English translation: *mettre, demander, sortir, écouter, regarder, rendre, chercher, jouer,* and *attendre.* The French verbs and the English equivalents are not similarly distributed in the constructions of the two languages (Politzer, 1965, ch. 8). For example:

    Il a mis son chapeau   *"He* put on *his hat"*
    Il attend sa femme   *"He is waiting for his wife"*

It has been the purpose of this article to outline a means of classifying French verbs according to their distribution in clause constructions. It was suggested that greater results might be obtained by helping the student focus on one pattern at a time. But merely separating the verbs according to their syntactic roles is not enough. Competent textbook writers must devise a pedagogically best order by which the structures could be presented. In addition to the verbs chosen, the actual sentences to be presented and drilled should employ the most frequent and useful nouns, adjectives, adverbs and grammatical words.

The lists of verbs in themselves are of little or no help to the beginning student. The verbs must be presented with those words which typically occur with the verbs. For example, in the tV$_2$ class, *écouter, aimer,* and *attendre* will often be found with a direct object which belongs to the animate class: *j'attends ma femme.* The direct object used after *manger, penser, travailler,* and *jouer* does not belong to the animate class.

Once the basic constructions are presented and drilled, the student has to be trained to communicate in a more natural fashion than is possible when he is limited to one structure. This is possibly best accomplished by having the students answer and ask a variety of questions by which they are forced to recall previously learned structures and to combine the material to form new utterances.

An interesting experiment with a monostructural approach in the teaching of French, German, and Spanish has been carried on at the University of Northern Iowa under the direction of Samuel Nodarse. New material is introduced in question-answer form through the use of the overhead projector. Each transparency is limited to one structure and consists of a series of questions and answers. Students repeat the pattern after the instructor. For example:

Jean travaille-t-il?   *Oui, Jean travaille*
Jean bavarde-t-il?   *Oui, Jean bavarde*

Extensive use is made of expansion-type drills through which the student adds to the basic structure by answering questions such as who?, what?, when?, where?, with whom?, etc. For example:

Jean travaille-t-il? Oui, Jean travaille
Où travaille-t-il? Il travaille en ville (à la campagne, etc.)
Quand travaille-t-il en ville? etc.
Avec qui . . . ? etc.

The above-mentioned experiment and other efforts to present material one structure at a time should be encouraged. The results will certainly have to be compared with those of other methods employed at the basic level before superiority can be claimed. It can however be claimed that, other things equal, students will learn French faster if they are able to grasp the pattern being presented. If it is true that the failure in the dialogue-oriented methods is caused by the effort to learn several patterns at one time, greater success can be hoped for in materials which employ a monostructural approach. The basic clauses and classes of verbs established in this article can possibly be of use to those interested in employing such an approach.

REFERENCES

Cook, Walter A. 1969. *Introduction to Tagmemic Analysis.* New York: Holt, Rinehart and Winston.

Dubois, Jean. 1967. *Grammaire structurale du français: le verbe.* Paris: Larousse.

Gougenheim, G. et al. 1964. *L'Elaboration du français fondamental.* Paris: Didier.

Grittner, Frank. 1969. *Teaching Foreign Languages.* New York: Harper and Row.

Longacre, Robert E. 1964. *Grammar Discovery Procedures.* The Hague: Mouton.

Martinet, André. 1969. *Le Français sans fard.* Paris: Presses Universitaires de France.

Moulton, William. 1970. *A Linguistic Guide to Language Learning.* New York: The Modern Language Association of America.

Oates, Michael D. 1970. "A Tagmemic Approach to Adverbial Classification in French" (unpublished Georgetown University Ph.D. dissertation).

Pike, Kenneth. 1967. *Language in Relation to a Unified Theory of the Structure of Human Behavior.* The Hague: Mouton.

Politzer, Robert. 1965. *Teaching French, An Introduction to Applied Linguistics.* Waltham, Massachusetts: Blaisdell.

Rivenc, Paul. 1968. "Lexique et langue parlée". *Le Français dans le Monde* 57, p. 25-33.

Valdman, Albert. 1966. *Trends in Language Teaching.* New York: McGraw-Hill.

ALBERT VALDMAN*

Language Variation and the
Teaching of French

1. THE STATIC MODEL OF LANGUAGE

Languages are widely variable. Little sophistication in linguistic analysis is required to observe readily instances of variation at all levels of language: phonological, grammatical, and lexical. For instance, some speakers of English pronounce the second vowel of *tomato* like the vowel of *mate* and others like that of *pot*. At the lexical level, what some call a *pail* is known to others as a *bucket*, and whereas some carry groceries in *bags* others prefer *sacks*. Yet in the past fifty years and more, linguists have operated with a static paradigm of language; they have described individual languages in terms of "an ideal speaker-listener in a completely homogeneous speech community (Chomsky, 1965:3)." Structural linguists who have dominated the linguistic scene during the last fifty years are not unaware of the inherent variability of the object of their study. But only if they assume that the speech of an individual speaker is homogeneous and that members of a monolingual speech community all speak alike can they describe a language:

> Pour simplifier notre analyse, nous supposerons que la langue qui
> évolue est celle d'une communauté strictement unilingue et
> homogène, dans le sens que les différences qu'on y pourrait constater
> ne correspondraient qu'aux stades successifs d'un même usage, et

---

* Indiana University—Bloomington

87

non à des usages concurrents. Ceci, bien entendu, ne correspond guère à la réalité telle qu'on l'observe . . . où s'enchevêtrent toutes sortes d'influences et où existent concurremment des usages d'origine sociale et géographique variée (Martinet, 1960:178).

Structural linguists have espoused—some of them in a very militant fashion—a strictly objective, descriptive attitude toward language. In other words, they have striven to report how people *do* speak, not how they *should* speak. But it is difficult not to slip into a normative or prescriptive attitude when one eliminates all variation and describes a language in terms of the ideal speaker-listener. In linguistic communities such as those that speak English or French, it is likely that the ideal speaker-listener will exhibit careful, monitored middle-class speech and may even lapse into formal if not archaic speech features. The inability of structural linguists to handle language variation within a static model has had several effects on language teaching.

First, it has led to a curious paradox. Since the early 1940's, a high value has been placed on audiolingual communicative behavior; yet the language of the ideal speaker-listener which has generally been selected for the preparation of audiolingual-oriented materials is hardly characteristic of the speech used in natural face-to-face communication, even among middle-class educated adults. And since most learners are adolescents and young adults, the language used in teaching materials is even less characteristic of spontaneous conversation among their counterparts in the target-language community.

Second, faced with the inherent variability of the language to be learned, language teachers and material developers have adopted one of two attitudes. They assumed that the learner would eventually acquire by osmosis, as it were, the native speaker's variable range. This approach has hardly been successful, and learners either fail to note variations or are confused by them. They form incorrect generalizations from raw data and are led to make errors. The other solution has been for the teacher or material developer to seek simplicity and symmetry in normative rules which do not accurately account for the speech to which students are exposed if they have the opportunity of hearing authentic native-speech samples.

This paper starts from the contention that the acquisition of near-native competence in a foreign language implies the ability to correctly interpret widely variable authentic native speech and to approximate the educated native speaker's ability to shift from one type of speech to another depending on the various sociolinguistic and psychological circumstances surrounding natural verbal communicative behavior. But at the beginning and intermediate levels, one must be satisfied with less than near-native competence, and it is the responsibility of material developers to prepare contrived samples of the foreign language which will exhibit less variation than natural speech in order that the beginning and intermediate learner be able to attain a reasonable degree of communicative competence. But the reduction of the inherent variability of natural speech cannot be effected arbitrarily, and one of the important areas of applied linguistics is the formulation of principles that will guide the production of fairly homogeneous speech which, at the same time, (1) will not offend educated speakers of the target language, (2) do not depart from those that characterize natural speech, (3) still reflect important generalities of the system underlying natural speech, (4) are readily learned, and (5) will not inhibit the ultimate acquisition of the full range of variation displayed by educated native speakers. These principles will be termed *pedagogical norms.* The notion of pedagogical norm will be illustrated in three areas of language structure: (1) in phonology, it will be applied to the problem of the mid-vowels; (2) in syntax, it will be applied to the choice from among the multiple synonymous interrogative structures; (3) in morphophonology, that part of the description of a language that deals with the phonological form of meaningful elements, it will be brought to bear on problems of liaison. Before I proceed to this three-fold illustration, I should like to underscore the difference between my approach and the traditional one.

Traditional grammarians and orthoepists impose a uniform usage which, they claim, represents that of educated speakers. No attempt is made to simplify the system for the beginning learner. A pedagogical norm does not claim to correspond exactly to the usage of educated speakers, although it is obviously based on that usage. More importantly, it is designed with the explicit purpose of facilitating the beginner's acquisition of the target language. The use of pedagogical norms also implies a more realistic attitude toward objectives of beginning and intermediate language instruction. If we expect learners at these levels to use the target language for communicative purposes, we must accept the fact that their control of the phonological and grammatical features will be less than near-native. In other words, if we wish beginning and intermediate students to engage in a significant amount of communicative use of language, we must be prepared to sacrifice some accuracy in their control of outward form.

2. La Loi de Position as a Pedagogical Norm

In their careful monitored style, educated Paris speakers, who constitute undeniably the prestige speakers of the language, differentiate six mid-vowels. The differentiative value of the six mid-vowels is demonstrated by the following *minimal pairs*, pairs of words or phrases with different meaning and differing by the segment under consideration:

le gué   [ge]   "the ford"   vs.   le guet   [gɛ]   "the watch"

jeûne   [ʒøn]   "fast"   vs.   jeune   [ʒœn]   "young"

le saule   [sol]   "the willow"   vs.   le sol   [sɔl]   "the ground"

The members of the three contrastive pairs [e] vs. [ɛ], [ø], vs. [œ], and [o] vs. [ɔ] differ by the fact that the first is produced with smaller mouth aperture (or higher tongue position) than the second. Another set of articulatory terms used to distinguish members of these pairs is close versus open (or lax).

But these contrasts do not always occur in all positions in words or phrases and are not always made by the same speaker in various circumstances or by speakers from various geographical regions or social levels. In fact, they are subject to at least five types of limitations or variations: (1) limitation of distribution within words; (2) neutralization in non-final position within words or phrases; (3) alternations within the speech of the same speakers influenced by morphological factors; (4) geographical variation; (5) social variation. These will be discussed in detail below.

2.1 Limitation of Distribution

The mid-vowels do not constitute as symmetrical a set as listings in articulatory charts might lead one to suppose, and it is more useful to distinguish the unrounded front vowels [e] and [ɛ] (which must be related to the long vowel [ɛ:]) from the rounded pairs [ø]/[œ] and [o]/[ɔ], see Table 1.

Table 1   Mid-Vowel Front and Rounded Vowel Systems

(Front)
Unrounded
Vowels

Rounded
Vowels

High-mid	e	
Low-mid	ɛ	ɛ:
	short	long

High-mid	ø	o
Low-mid	œ	ɔ
	front	back

The differences between the unrounded pair and the rounded pairs are clearly brought out when one considers the occurrence or *distribution* of the individual vowels in the last syllable of words. The front unrounded close vowel [e] does not occur in *closed* syllables, that is, syllables that end with a consonant, whereas its open partner [ɛ] occurs freely in both types of final syllables. For the rounded vowels, the open vowels [ɔ] and [œ] do not occur in *open* syllables, that is, syllables that end with a vowel. Both close and open rounded vowels occur in closed syllables, but the former are subject to more limitations, see Table 2.

TABLE 2 DISTRIBUTION OF THE SIX MID-VOWEL PHONEMES RELATIVE TO WORD-FINAL BOUNDARY AND PERMISSIBLE FINAL CONSONANTS

Environ-ment	Vowel					
	e	ɛ	ɔ	o	œ	∅
Open syllable						
−#	poignée	poignet	x	peau	x	peau
Closed syllable						
−C						
ʒ	(aurai-je)	aurai-je	loge	l'auge	x	(Maubeuge)
t		sept	hotte	hôte	x	(meute)
z		pèse	x	pause	x	creuse
d		raide	rode	rôde	x	(Eudes)
l		sel	sol	saule	veulent	(veule)
n		benne	bonne	Beaune	jeune	(jeûne)
f		chef	étoffe	sauf	bœuf	x
v		lève	love	mauve	peuvent	x
r		serre	sort	x	sœur	x
j		oreille	x	x	feuille	x
p		guêpe	tope	taupe	x	x
b		plèbe	robe	aube	x	x
k		sec	roc	rauque	x	x
s		caisse	cosse	causse	x	x
ʃ		pêche	poche	embauche	x	x
m		aime	homme	heaume	x	x
g		bègue	vogue	x	x	x
ɲ		règne	grogne	x	x	x

2.2 NEUTRALIZATION IN NON-FINAL SYLLABLES

In non-final position the distinction between close and open mid-vowels is said to be *neutralized* for each of the three pairs. While educated Paris speakers are able to distinguish such minimal pairs as:

les sons	[lesõ]	vs.	laissons	[lɛsõ]
ceux-là	[søla]	vs.	cela	[sœla]
fausser	[fose]	vs.	fossé	[fɔse]

in careful, monitored speech, they often will use a vowel intermediate between close and open in normal speech. Indeed, Paris speakers will usually not clearly distinguish between *l'office* and *le fils* in normal style since they use a vowel whose timbre is close to that of [ə] in the first syllable of both phrases.

2.3 MORPHOPHONOLOGICAL ALTERNATIONS (ANALOGY)

Traditional descriptions state that the mid-vowel used in non-final syllables of words is often determined by analogy with forms that are morphologically related. Consider the sets *saut, sautes, sauter, sauterie*, on the one hand, and *sot, sotte, sottise, sottement*, on the other. Since the forms containing the morphological element *saut-* "jump" are always pronounced with [o], it is much more likely that polysyllabic forms such as *sauter* and *sauterie* will be pronounced with the same vowel rather than the neutral vowel [ə] one often hears in normal-style pronunciations of such words as *aumônier, mauvais, lauréat* which have no monosyllabic morphologically related forms. Forms containing the morphological element *sot-* "stupid" are pronounced [o] (*sot*) and [ɔ] (*sotte*) in monosyllabic words, and in polysyllabic forms such as *sottise* and *sottement* they are likely to be pronounced with a [ɔ] that is less likely to become neutralized to [ə] than that of such words as *société, politique, solitude*. Thus the pronunciation of polysyllabic words with monosyllabic morphologically related forms is subject to considerable variation (*flottement*): *aimer* may be pronounced with a neutral front unrounded mid-vowel [E] or with [ɛ], on the basis of the analogy with *aime; heureux* may be pronounced with a vowel similar in timbre to that of [ø] or with [œ], on the basis of the analogy with *bonheur.*

2.4 GEOGRAPHICAL DIALECT VARIATION

Speakers of French from all sections of Southern France do not generally distinguish between members of the three mid-vowel pairs. In other words, they cannot differentiate such minimal pairs as *gué/ guet, jeûne/jeune*, or *saule/sol* on the basis of pronunciation alone. But this does not mean they can produce only three mid-vowels. Indeed, they normally produce six mid-vowel timbres but distribute them in such a way that only one occurs normally in any particular environment. In open syllables, they use a close vowel: *guet, gué* [ge]; *deux* [dø]; *dos* [do]. In closed syllables they use only an open vowel: *belle* [bɛl]; *heureuse* [ørœz]; *gauche* [gɔʃ]. As they do not occur in the same environment, the close and open members of each pair cannot contrast, see Table 3.

TABLE 3   DISTRIBUTION OF MID-VOWELS IN SOUTHERN (MÉRIDIONAL)
ACCENTED STANDARD FRENCH

	open syllable	closed syllable
e	gué, guet	————
ɛ	————	guèpe
ø	peut	————
œ	————	peuvent, menteuse
o	saut	————
ɔ	————	sotte, sautes

There are other variations in the mid-vowel system determined by regional dialect differences. Speakers from various parts of Northern France do not distinguish between [e] and [ɛ] in final position and are likely to replace [ɛ] by [e] in such words as *bouquet, vrai, je vais, il était;* others use a vowel approximating [ɛ] instead of [e] in such words as *été, dernier, cheminée;* still others use a close vowel instead of the open vowel in such words as *sol* and *seul.*

2.5 SOCIAL DIALECT VARIATION

It is often stated that the speech of speakers from the lower and working classes exhibits the tendency toward the reduction of mid-vowels from six to three. Except for Southern France, where the simpler system of three distinctions but six phonetically distinct vowels is indeed more prevalent among non-middle-class speakers, there does not appear to be any simplification of the mid-vowel system that coincides clearly with social class membership. The pronunciation of such grammatically distinct forms as those of the 1st person singular of the future and the conditional and the past definite and past indefinite among working-class Paris speakers is particularly instructive.

Carefully documented studies show that working-class speakers in the Paris area do not distinguish between, say, *j'irai/j'irais* or *je parlai/je parlais.* But they do not replace [ɛ] by [e] in the conditional and imperfect as would Southern French speakers; they replace [e] by [ɛ] in the future and in the past definite. These speakers regularly differentiate such minimal pairs as *gué/guet* and thus have a consistent [e]/[ɛ] contrast.

2.6 THE LOI DE POSITION AS A PEDAGOGICAL NORM

The state of affairs characteristic of Southern French has been described by a broad generalization termed, rather inappropriately, *la Loi de Position*. The *Loi de Position* states that a mid-vowel is open in a closed syllable but closed in an open syllable, see Table 3. Some phoneticians have claimed that the *Loi de Position* reflects a tendency inherent in the French vowel system and one that would have reshaped the present-day vowel system had the development of the language not been disturbed by such external influences as the writing system and prescriptive orthoepists (Malmberg 1941:245). But we have seen that careful observation of the pronunciation variants of non-middle-class speakers who, one would expect, are less subject to the effect of the prescriptive tradition clearly shows that such is not at all the case. Nonetheless, the *Loi de Position* can serve as the basis of a useful pedagogical norm for the pronunciation of words containing mid-vowels.

First, would pronunciation habits characterized by the *Loi de Position* be acceptable to educated speakers and are they typical of their normal conversation style? Here a distinction must be made between the unrounded and the rounded vowels. The use of [e] in words for which [ɛ] is prescribed (*lait, carnet, quai, j'irais, j'allais,* etc.) is widespread among all types of French speakers and would not offend educated speakers. But the use of open rounded mid-vowels where close ones are prescribed would be readily observed by educated speakers and, in the mouth of foreign speakers, would elicit unfavorable reactions. The *Loi de Position* would need to be modified as follows: with regard to the pair [e]/[ɛ], use any of the two timbres or any intermediate timbre in non-final position; in final position, use the open vowel [ɛ] in closed syllables (*l'air, belle, sec*) and the close vowel [e] in open syllables, (*quai, carnet, lait, j'irais, j'allais*). For the rounded mid-vowels, the *Loi de Position* accurately describes the state of affairs in Standard French where the close vowels [œ] and [ɔ] do not occur. But the student would have to learn to use both the open and the close vowel in closed syllables. It might be objected that this would scarcely meet another of the five criteria for a pedagogical norm, namely, that it simplify the task of the beginning learner. From the point of view of pedagogical simplicity, the pedagogical norm becomes less and less useful the more one departs from the principle: open syllable = close vowel/closed syllable = open vowel, and the student is forced to memorize the particular vowel to be used in individual lexical items.

But in how many lexical items normally encountered by beginning students does the *Loi de Position* not hold for rounded vowels? I have examined the 3124 words of the *Français fondamental* list. A total of 36 words contained [ø] in closed final syllables and 18 contained [o] in that environment. But more importantly, all of the occurrences of [ø] were in the feminine form of adjectives ending in *eux*, e.g., *peureuse, paresseuse*, etc. Of the 18 occurrences of [o] in final closed syllables, five were also before a final [z]: *cause, chose, dispose, propose, repose*. The pedagogical norm would then need to be accompanied by a list of 13 items containing [o] in closed syllables ending with a consonant other than [z]: *côte, faute, haute, saute; fausse, grosse, sauce; sauf, chauve, pauvre, chaude, gauche, jaune*.

It cannot be objected that the use of the pedagogical norm outlined above would lead to the internalization of pronunciation habits which are incorrect and which would need to be replaced in later stages of instruction. The partial complementation between open and close mid-vowels which it describes is found in all varieties of French and in this way the pedagogical norm expresses a very important deep-seated generalization about the French vowel system. From the point of view of pedagogical simplicity, the pedagogical norm has much to recommend it. It can be stated to serve as a simple mnemonic device: open syllable = close vowel/closed syllable = open vowel. In very early stages of instruction, it is no doubt possible to contrive material so that no violations of the simplest form of the pedagogical norm are found. Any items such as *heureuse, chose, gauche*, etc. which violate the norm can be treated as individual exceptions. When a sufficiently large number of items ending in [z] have been encountered, a sub-generalization about closed syllables ending in [z] can be made.

3. CHOICE OF INTERROGATIVE STRUCTURE

Perhaps one of the most important and useful aspects of a foreign learner's proficiency in French is the ability to interpret and pose questions. Yet the structure of questions is an aspect of the grammar of French that is particularly troublesome because of extensive *synonymy*. Synonymy is here used in a non-technical sense to mean that to form questions, speakers of French have available several constructions which have the same meaning; that is, that express the same concepts. Consider sentences (1)-(5) below and pronominalized sentences that correspond to them:

(1) Où va Jean?   Où va-t-il?

(2) Où Jean va-t-il?   Lui, où va-t-il?

(3) Où est-ce que Jean va?   Où est-ce qu'il va?

(4) Jean va où?   Il va où?

(5) *Où Jean va?   ?Où il va?

The asterisk preceding sentence (5) indicates that it is not accepted as well-formed by most speakers of French and the question mark preceding the pronominalized version of (5) indicates that many speakers of French would express doubts about its well-formedness.

All five types of interrogative constructions convey the same meaning, and the use of any one type in a given situation is determined by stylistic and sociolinguistic considerations. In other words, these synonymous constructions have the same denotation but different connotations. When queried about the use of these constructions, educated speakers of French will generally assert that the type illustrated by (1) or (2), INV(ERSION) is the most correct and elegant but they will admit to using the type illustrated by (3) EST CE QUE with a high degree of frequency. They will also claim that they seldom use the types illustrated by (4), QU PRO(NOMINALIZA-TION) and (5), QU FRONTING, and will characterize them as either ill-formed or "vulgar," "low class," etc. But in fact a study of the *Français fondamental* corpus (Pottier 1964) shows that EST CE QUE constitutes about 75 per cent of questions containing question words (QU) and that the next most frequent type was QU PRO. With regard to QU FRONTING, it is found extensively in regional dialects and in child language. For instance, it would be rather anomalous for a child to ask another child's name by saying *Comment t'appelles-tu?* instead of *Comment tu t'appelles?*

Thus, teachers and material developers are confronted with a serious problem in the selection and the ordering of French interrogative structures, for several synonymous constructions are also available for simple yes/no questions:

(1a) *Va Jean à Paris?   Va-t-il à Paris?
(2a) Jean va-t-il à Paris?   Lui, va-t-il à Paris?
(3a) Est-ce que Jean va à Paris? Est-ce qu'il va à Paris?
(4a) Jean va à Paris?   Il va à Paris?

Type (4a), which is usually termed SIMPLE INTONATION CHANGE corresponds to (4) where the sentence element questioned is simply replaced by the appropriate interrogative pronominal. Most textbooks seem blithely unaware of the problem and it is not unusual to find all four types of yes/no questions presented in the introductory lessons of materials destined for beginning students. As a rule, only INV and EST CE QUE types of QU questions (questions containing an interrogative pronominal, such as *Où va-t-il, Que fait-il*, etc.) are introduced in beginning and intermediate texts, but without any apparent ordering. I suggest that to force students to manipulate synonymous constructions is to needlessly multiply their difficulties and to retard acquisition on their part of the ability to communicate effectively in French. In this section of my article I will show that, in addition, it is counter-intuitive in that it does not correspond to what language learners do when they acquire a language without the assistance (or the interference) of the teacher or the textbook, and I should like to discuss criteria that should guide the selection and the ordering of synonymous question types in French. I will deal with QU questions, although the conclusions I reach apply also to yes/no questions.

3.1 FREQUENCY

There are no extensive studies of the relative frequency of the five question types presented above in the various styles of speech of educated speakers. However, as has been noted in the preceding section, available studies indicate that EST CE QUE is the most frequent by far, followed by QU PRO and INV.

3.2 SOCIOLINGUISTIC ACCEPTABILITY

The fact that educated speakers of French consider QU PRO and, particularly, QU FRONTING ill-formed or substandard is of great significance for the teacher of French as a foreign language. As was the case for the mid-vowels, we will need to eliminate from comparison constructions which are deemed ill-formed or substandard, even though the speakers making these judgments use these on numerous occasions. It is a useful guideline to require foreign learners to speak "better" than native speakers; that is, to use a dialect and styles characteristic of the formal, monitored speech of educated native speakers. On the other hand, it is important that the foreign learner, as he progresses in the study of the language, be able to recognize features found in the spontaneous speech of educated speakers as well as in that of speakers in geographical areas or from social levels that show marked deviation from the prestige dialect. In fact, one of the features that marks off the highly proficient foreign learner from the native speaker is precisely the ability to adjust to geographically and socially determined variations in speech. These considerations are particularly important in the area of listening comprehension. Thus, sociolinguistic considerations would lead us to identify INV and EST CE QUE as the two interrogative types to be presented to beginning and intermediate students for active mastery, but the relatively high frequency of use of QU PRO by educated speakers suggests that it should be taught for passive recognition despite the fact that educated speakers are not conscious of the high frequency of their use

of this construction in spontaneous conversation and may even consider it substandard. While a native speaker's overt comments about
sociolinguistic aspects of his speech constitute important linguistic
data, they do not necessarily reflect his actual linguistic behavior
inasmuch as the latter is strongly influenced by his society's attitude
toward permissible variation in speech behavior. As the famous dic-
tum "Dans le cœur de tout français, il y a un grammairien qui som-
meille" suggests, there exists in France a strong normative and
prescriptive tradition about speech features which are acceptable for
middle-class linguistic behavior, and it exerts a powerful influence on
all speakers who aspire to middle-class status.

3.3 STRUCTURAL COMPLEXITY

It is difficult to assess the degree of relative complexity of a given
grammatical construction for a particular learner since it is determined by a variety of psychological as well as structural factors. In
this section, I will attempt to compare only the relative structural
complexity of the synonymous QU question types: INV, EST CE
QUE, QU PRO, and QU FRONTING. I will use a transformational
framework for this comparison, although I do not claim that the
transformations I posit are well motivated within a formal overall
generative-transformational treatment of French syntax[1] nor that the
sentence type to which the transformations apply represents the correct deep structure.

Assume that we wish to question the direct object of a sentence,
and that furthermore we refer to a thing (inanimate). We start from
a sentence like:

(6) Il prend + Direct Object (inanimate)

The first step in the formulation of the appropriate question is to provide the required QU pronoun, and its output is a question of the
QU PRO type:

(7) Il prend *quoi?*

which is well formed and in fact very frequent in spontaneous conversational French.

The next step is to move the QU pronoun to the front of the sentence, which generates the question of the QU FRONTING type:

(8) *Quoi il prend?

which, however, is not well-formed. First, a morphophonemic change
quoi → *que/qu'* is required since *quoi* is not permitted in unstressed

---

[1] For a generative-transformational derivation of French interrogative
constructions, see: Langacker 1965, 1971; Hirschbühler 1970; Roulet
1969.

(final) position. Second, only certain types of interrogative pronominals may be fronted without accompanying syntactic changes:

(9) Pourquoi tu dis ça?

(10) Comment il s'appelle?

The INV and EST CE QUE types of questions require the preceding application of both QU PRO and QU FRONTING and are more complex structurally than these two types. INV requires in addition the inversion of the subject and the verb and EST CE QUE the insertion of the formative *est-ce que*[2] after the QU pronominal:

(11) Que prend-il?

(12) Qu'est-ce qu'il prend?

A scale of relative structural complexity difficulty ranges is obtained by counting the number of transformations that need to be applied in deriving a given question type from the basic sentence, see Table 4.

TABLE 4   SCALE OF RELATIVE STRUCTURAL COMPLEXITY OF SYNONYMOUS QUESTION TYPES

Transformations Applied	Question Type			
	QU PRO	QU FRONTING	INV	EST CE QUE
Qu Pronominal	x	x	x	x
Qu Fronting		x	x	x
Inversion			x	(x)
Est-ce que insertion				x

If we consider that inversion has been applied to derive *est-ce que* from *c'est que*, the EST CE QUE type appears to be the most structurally complex question type.

3.4 EXTENSIVITY, PRODUCTIVITY AND GENERALITY

It was pointed out in Section 3.3 that QU FRONTING can be applied without additional syntactic changes only if the sentence contains certain QU pronominals. In this section, I should like to compare the constraints that apply to the INV and the EST CE QUE question types, which, as was shown in Section 3.2, are accepted by educated speakers as always correct. From a pedagogical point of

---

[2] Langacker 1965 suggests that EST CE QUE questions are in fact derived by embedding the interrogative sentence in a *c'est* + complement clause and then applying the subject-verb inversion to the dominating clause. This would result in *c'est que* → *est-ce que*. This derivation is challenged by Roulet 1969.

view, the more constraints apply to a linguistic feature, the more difficult it is to teach since each constraint corresponds to an exception that limits the generality of the main rule. Consider first EST CE QUE. For the English learner QU PRO and QU FRONTING which must precede the insertion of *est-ce que* do not present any special problems, since they correspond to transformations that must be applied to derive corresponding English questions:

    (13) What do you do?

    (14) Where is he going?

In addition, when the direct object is questioned in English, a distinction must also be made between animate and inanimate:

    (15) What did he see?   Il a vu quoi?

    (16) Whom (who) did he see?   Il a vu qui?

All the student need do, then, is to insert *est-ce* or *est-ce qu'* before the subject:

    (17) Qu'*est-ce qu'*il dit?

    (18) Où *est-ce que* Jean va?

    (19) Pourquoi *est-ce que* tu as fait ça?

But whereas inversion always yields correct questions if the subject is a pronoun:

    (20) Quand partira-t-il?

    (21) Qu'a-t-il pris?

the inversion of a subject containing a noun produces in certain cases ill-formed or dubious sentences:

    (22) ?Quand partira Jean?

    (23) *Qu'a Jean pris?

    (24) *Pourquoi ne répondra pas votre frère?

In particular, it is impossible to use INV in questions which question a subject containing an inanimate noun. That is, although the following are acceptable:

    (25) Qui fait du bruit?   Qui est-ce qui fait du bruit?

(answer: *Les enfants font du bruit,* or *Le bébé fait du bruit?*), only EST CE QUE can be used in (26):

    (26) *Que fait du bruit?   Qu'est-ce qui fait du bruit?

(answer: *Le moteur fait du bruit*).

    Indeed, it is necessary in a proper syntactic description of French to posit several inversion transformations.[3] The only inversion transformation that is properly interrogative is that which inverts a subject pronoun and the following verb. The inversion of a subject containing a noun is not an exclusive feature of interrogative sentences:

---

[3] See Kayne 1971.

(27) La voiture qu'a vue *mon frère* est plus belle que la vôtre.
(27a) La voiture que *mon frère* a vue est plus belle que la vôtre.
In view of the severe constraints that apply to the application of subject-verb inversion in interrogative sentences, mastery of the INV question type for active production requires a longer period of training than does that of the EST CE QUE type, and the foreign learner of French who wishes to use it is more likely to make errors than if he chose EST CE QUE. It should also be pointed out that most of the constraints that apply to INV in QU question also apply to yes/no questions:

(29) Partira-t-il?   *Partira Jean?
(30) A-t-il chanté?   *A Jean chanté? or *A chanté Jean?

3.5 Contrastive Analysis

Many applied linguists and methodologists believe that the more a feature of the target language (French, in this case) differs from that of the native language (English), the more it is difficult to acquire. This belief has led to extensive point-by-point comparison of two languages in order to identify points of conflict or interference and to assess the relative difficulty of the acquisition of target language features. Without passing any judgment on the correctness or adequacy of the contrastive view, I would like to again compare INV and EST CE QUE, although it will become apparent that relative difference with respect to corresponding native-language features is the most difficult criterion to evaluate.

Compare sentences (31) and (32) below:

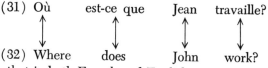

(31) Où   est-ce que   Jean   travaille?

(32) Where   does   John   work?

Note that in both French and English *est-ce que* and the form of *do* can be considered introduced by interrogation[4] and that, furthermore, there is a one-to-one relationship between corresponding elements of the two languages. The same isomorphy exists for English questions containing a semantically full modal auxiliary verb:

---

[4] Of course, *do* insertion is not a feature used exclusively in interrogative sentences. It must apply to any emphatic, negative or interrogative sentence in English which does not contain a modal auxiliary or the verbs *have* or *be:*

I run	I *didn't* run
He works	He *does* work.
We sang.	*Did* we sing?

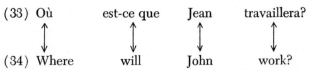

(33) Où   est-ce que   Jean   travaillera?

(34) Where   will   John   work?

On the other hand, the isomorphy is broken if we compare French INV questions and their English equivalents:

(35) Où   ———   travaille   Jean?

(36) Where   does   John   work?

In (35) and (36), only the interrogative pronominals occur in the same position in the sentence. In the other variant of the INV question type

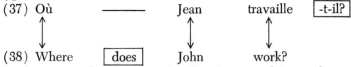

(37) Où   ———   Jean   travaille   -t-il?

(38) Where   does   John   work?

there is better matching, except for the elements that can be considered to be introduced in the sentence by interrogation, *does* in English and the reduplicated and pronominalized subject pronoun *t-il* in *French*.

To conclude this section, it appears that EST CE QUE should be more easily acquired by English learners of French since it results in a close one-to-one matching between semantically equivalent elements of corresponding sentences in the two languages.

3.6 Observation of Student Errors

The five criteria I have discussed point to the fact that EST CE QUE type questions should be taught first and drilled and manipulated exclusively until students have acquired firm mastery of them. Before I make concrete suggestions for the gradual introduction of the other question types after EST CE QUE is under complete control by the student, I should like to present data that indicate that students find it too costly in using a foreign language to operate with synonymous constructions and restructure the language data to which they are exposed in a way that reduces grammatical constraints and enables them to communicate effectively, if not always elegantly or in an error-free manner.

Unfortunately, the dominance of interference theory and reliance on contrastive analysis that claimed to predict learning problems a priori have diverted the attention of applied linguistics and methodologists from careful observation of the actual process of second-language acquisition. Thus there have been no major studies of natural language learning nor systematic observation of errors made by students in academic language learning. There currently is a growing interest in this area (Corder 1967; Richards 1970), no doubt stemming from the rationalist theory of first-language acquisition. It will be recalled that proponents of this theory claim that human beings have an innate, genetically determined propensity for language learning and that the most important feature of first-language acquisition is not direct imitation of parental speech but the construction on the part of the child of a successive set of grammars gradually approximating adult grammar from raw language data. The adaptation of this model of language learning to adolescent and adult second-language learning would posit that, when their natural language-learning strategies are allowed to operate without external interference, such as that of the teacher, these learners restructure foreign-language data into simpler systems which they can then handle better in the communication of meaningful linguistic messages. For proponents of this view, learning errors are crucial in devising appropriate teaching materials and methods, for they reveal the strategies which learners find most effective and economical.

To test this view, I elicited QU questions from a student who had studied French for two years at the high-school level but had subsequently spent a summer in France and had had the opportunity to react with French speakers of her own age. Here is a sample of the QU questions she produced during the interview. The data were elicited by presenting a situation in English and asking the subject to formulate the appropriate question in French, for example sentence (39) was elicited by asking: "Suppose you wanted to ask a good friend of yours where she was going, what would you say?":

INV

(39) Où vas-tu?
(40) Où travaillez-vous?
(41) Où travaille Jean?
(42) Pour qui travaille Jean?
(43) Qui voyez-vous?

EST CE QUE

(44) Qu'est-ce que vous mangez?
(45) Qu'est-ce que vous */vwa/?
(46) Qu'est-ce que vous aimez?

QU FRONTING

(47) *Quand vous *partir?
(48) Quand vous *a parti?

(49) ?A quelle heure vous mangez?

(50) ?Pourquoi vous dites ça?

(51) A quelle heure vous êtes parti?

It is interesting to note that the subject made use of three QU question types: INV, EST CE QUE, and QU FRONTING. But note that these are not viewed as synonymous, on the contrary, there is a clear complementation in their use:

(i)   INV is used primarily to question the adverbial of place;

(ii) EST CE QUE is used to question inanimate direct objects, and it appears that the subject has equated *what* and *qu'est-ce que;*

(iii) QU FRONTING has the widest domain of use among the three question types. It is particularly interesting to note that only with inversion does the subject show full control of 2nd person plural verb forms.

One might ask how the learner has reconstructed QU FRONTING questions from the random samples of French to which she was exposed. It is unlikely that even younger French speakers would make such a preponderant use of that construction. One might posit the following process. The subject was exposed massively to the QU PRO type (e.g., *Tu vas où?, Tu vas partir quand?*) which is no doubt very frequent in the speech of adolescents and younger adults. Since she had no exposure to that type during her formal study of French, she was forced to analyze it in terms of the two question types she had learned and English interrogative structures. In all these types of questions, the QU is fronted, so she fronted the QU but retained the normal subject and verb order of the QU PRO type.

3.7 SOME PEDAGOGICAL SUGGESTIONS

The five criteria I have discussed and the preliminary observation of restructuring of French QU questions on the part of an English-speaking learner suggest the following principles for the selection and the ordering of these synonymous constructions.

The first QU question type to be introduced should be EST CE QUE. In beginning stages, it should be used exclusively both for passive and active acquisition except for a small set of fixed locutions to be taught as individual lexical items such as *Comment vous appelez-vous?, Quelle heure est-il?, Quel temps fait-il?* To try to replace these locutions with EST CE QUE would result in artificial sentences: *?Comment est-ce que vous vous appelez?, ?Quelle heure est-ce qu'il est?* Note however that the use of *est-ce que* is quite natural in sentences with related meaning: *Comment est-ce que tu vas?, A quelle heure est-ce que vous partez?*

Second, INV is introduced for reading comprehension but only in sentences whose subject contains a pronoun: *Que dit-il?*, or a noun phrase plus a pronominalized reduplicated subject: *Quand le train part-il?* In this way, the student does not run the risk of overgeneralizing subject-verb inversion in sentences containing a noun as subject: *Quand part le train* but **Quand est parti le train?* (whose correct INV form is *Quand le train est-il parti?*).

Third, at the intermediate level, students are led to manipulate and acquire active mastery of INV questions whose subject is a pronoun.

Fourth, QU PRO is introduced for passive acquisition. Since this construction is characteristic of spontaneous speech, students should have the opportunity of learning to recognize it in authentic recorded texts. Finally, students should be exposed to completely unedited authentic recorded texts which will show the entire set of QU question types, but they should still be encouraged to limit themselves to EST CE QUE and INV when they produce French utterances.

With regard to QU questions where the subject is the questioned element, there are two variant types if the subject is animate:

(53) Qui a pris mes livres?   or
(54) Qui est-ce qui a pris mes livres?

EST CE QUE must be used where the questioned subject is inanimate or indeterminate:

(55) Qu'est-ce qui est tombé
(56) Qu'est-ce qui se passe?

For the sake of symmetry it would be preferable to teach the EST CE QUE variant. But since questions bearing on inanimate subjects are relatively rare, the choice of variant in this area is not crucial.

4. Liaison and Elision

Probably the linguistic feature that makes French relatively difficult for foreigners to master is the alternation in the spoken form of many words subsumed under the traditional terms *liaison* and *elision*. Liaison may be defined as the alternation between the loss and retention of the final consonant of words, and therefore also includes alternations in the form of verbs and adjectives which are not grouped under liaison in traditional analyses of French. But note that there is no difference in the following alternations:

un ami [œ̃n ami]	un camarade [œ̃ kamarad]
bon hôtel [bɔn otɛl]	bon restaurant [bõ rɛstɔrã]
premier étage [prəmjɛr eta ʒ]	premier couloir [premje kulwar]
ils ont [ilz õ]	ils sont [il sõ]

From the point of view of spoken French, liaison is not merely the "linking" of a consonant to the next word but the presence or loss of the final consonant of a word sometimes accompanied by changes in vowels that take place across grammatical and word boundaries. In the teaching of French, a distinction must be made between obligatory liaison (*liaison obligatoire*) and optional liaison (*liaison facultative*). It would seem that the former is best handled as a grammatical phenomenon, that is, the way adjective and verb inflection are handled. Just as the learner learns that *petit* [pti] is used with masculine nouns and *petite* [ptit] with feminine nouns or that *vient* [vjɛ̃] is used with third person singular present indicative and *viennent* [vjɛn] with third person plural, so he should learn that [pti] is used before words beginning with a consonant or at the end of a phrase but [ptit] before words beginning with a vowel or that [il] is used before words beginning with a consonant and [ilz] before words beginning with a vowel.[5] By classifying these features under pronunciation problems, teachers of French underestimate the amount of practice that is required before the learner can acquire active mastery.

At the source of the inadequate treatment of liaison in many textbooks is a confusion between liaison as a phenomenon of the spoken language and the representation of liaison consonants by French spelling. Since all instances of liaison, obligatory and optional, are represented in spelling by a final consonant letter, no distinction is usually made between teaching the two types. And liaison is interpreted simply as the linking of final consonants to the word that follows:

(57) Les‿enfants ont‿essayé deux‿autres‿exercices.

But pronouncing liaison consonants when reading French sentences and pronouncing or deleting final consonants when producing spoken sentences in a meaningful context are two different activities, the latter being much more difficult than the former. And it is clear that the memorization of a set of liaison rules and reading aloud sentences will not lead to effective spoken control of obligatory liaison.

To return to the problem of language variation proper, the teacher needs to provide clear guidelines in the pronunciation or deletion of optional liaison consonants. In this area, educated French speakers exhibit a behavior that can be characterized as nearly random. And thus, from a pedagogical point of view, the most efficient solution is to require students to make as few optional liaisons as possible. In ef-

---

[5] In spontaneous conversational French, *ils* is pronounced [i] before a consonant and [iz] before a vowel.

fect, it means that so far as their productive repertory is concerned there is only obligatory liaison. That is, no distinction is made between the liaisons of

(58) les_amis

and

(59) ils sont_jci

although French speakers will link the [z] of (58) in 100 per cent of the cases but that of (59) in only 75 per cent, say. In addition to an exhaustive inventory of obligatory liaison, applied linguists need to provide data on the relative frequency of optional liaison in texts representative of a variety of styles of educated French speakers. It could then be decided on a cut-off percentage figure, say, 75 per cent, above which optional liaisons would be treated as obligatory in the formulation of pedagogical norms.

The same procedure needs to be applied to the more vexing problem of the elision of mute e, so that in his production of French sentences the learner will be guided by a small number of simple rules which determine a style of speech perfectly acceptable to educated speakers but which reduce a large part of the variation inherent in the normal use of a language by an heterogeneous speech community. As in the case of the mid-vowels and interrogative structures, the learner must also be introduced gradually to authentic samples of natural speech showing uncontrolled variation so that, whereas his productive inventory will differ from that of native speakers by its greater homogeneity, his receptive inventory will match theirs, as will his ability to understand natural speech.

REFERENCES

Chomsky, Noam. 1967. *Aspects of a Theory of Syntax*. Cambridge, Mass.: M.I.T. Press.
Corder, S. Pitt. 1967. "The Significance of Learner's Errors." *International Review of Applied Linguistics* 5: 161-170.
Hirschbühler, Paul. 1970. *Traitement transformationnel de l'interrogation et quelques problèmes connexes en français*. (Dissertation, Université Libre de Bruxelles.)
Kayne, Richard S. 1971. "The Evolution of French Interrogatives." *Proceedings of the University of Florida Symposium on Generative-Transformational Grammar and the Romance Languages* (forthcoming).
Malmberg, Bertil. 1941. "Observations sur le système vocalique du français." *Acta Linguistica* 2: 234-46.

Martinet, André. 1960. *Eléments de linguistique générale.* Paris: Colin.
Richards, Jack A. 1970. *A Non-Causative Approach to Error Analysis.*
   Center for Research on Bilingualism, Laval University.
Roulet, Eddy. 1969. *Syntaxe de la proposition nucléaire en français
   parlé.* Brussels: AIMAV.